Call Me Jeanne

From Outhouse to the White House: A Journey of Family, Loss and the Power of Love

Jeanne Cahill

Colorful Crow
Publishing

Praise for *Call Me Jeanne*

"This is a fascinating memoir of a woman growing up in the South during a time of tremendous change! I look forward to reading the rest."
—**Carrie N. Baker**, J.D. Ph.D.

"How true it is that when an elder dies, a library is lost. The good news is that Jeanne Cahill, an elder indeed, has recorded her library, her memories, here in *Call Me Jeanne*. As a witness to so much of life that the rest of us call history, her life story provides a signpost for those of us who follow behind her."
—**Fran Stewart**, National best-selling author of the *Scot Shop Mysteries, Biscuit McKee Mysteries* and *After I Die: What My Executor Will Need to Know*

"*In Call Me Jeanne*, readers are invited into the vivid and remarkable life of Jeanne Cahill, a true Southern gem whose story spans nearly a century of history, change, and personal triumph. From her beginnings in South Georgia to her influential roles as a political activist, businessowner, and mother of three clever Cahills. Through her eloquent and heartfelt storytelling, Jeanne's memoir offers an unflinching look at her journey and the efforts of many to keep America an equitable place."
—**Jack Meyer**

"Jeanne Cahill doesn't hold anything back but shares the most personal details of her journey, creating a rich and inspiring narrative. This may be the most honest and authentic memoir you will ever read. This sweeping and engaging story of the life journey (so far) of 92-year-old Jeanne Cahill of Atlanta, Georgia, is a powerful and personal look at one woman's rise from a modest childhood and failed marriage to a successful life as a happily married mother, business owner and political activist. She mingled with the most prominent people in the country yet never lost her identity as a country girl from Georgia."

—**James A. Autry**, Author of *The Servant Leader*

"Jeanne Cahill is a gifted storyteller born of the same fertile South Georgia soil as Harry Crews and Caroline Pafford Miller. In sharing her remarkable life, Cahill invites us to travel with her through an intimate history of time and place, guiding us with equal parts of courage and delight. And indeed, we are most fortunate to be her companions on the journey."

—**Jonathan Hershey**, Ph.D., Professor of English and Writing, Georgia Highlands College

"Jeanne Cahill's engaging memoir documents an amazing life, from Depression-era farmgirl in South Georgia to proto-feminist to Jimmy Carter confidant to activist to entrepreneur. Warmly told with an eye for detail and an open heart, *Call Me Jeanne* brims with love of family and inspires with the tenacious spirit of its author."

—**Holly George-Warren**, author of *Janis: Her Life and Music* and coauthor of *Behind the Seams: My Life in Rhinestones* (with Dolly Parton)

"In her debut memoir, 92-year-old Jeanne Cahill, a remarkable Southern writer, takes readers on an extraordinary journey through her life. From growing up in the rural South
during the Great Depression to being appointed by President Carter to oversee pivotal committees on women's issues,
Jeanne's life story is a testament to resilience and dedication.
Her engaging and brilliant storytelling, infused with a unique-
ly Southern charm, vividly holds each chapter of her life up
to the light. This literary masterpiece is a captivating and inspiring account of a life well-lived, told by a voice that is both
authentic and profoundly moving."
—**Ray Waters**, Founder, The Village Church, Atlanta

"Lucid, gracious, delightfully humorous and unsparingly
honest, Jeanne Cahill's reflections on nearly a century of struggle, service, and resilience produce an inspiring portrait of
personal growth, social mobility, and political progress. Alight
with a generous and humble spirit, *Call Me Jeanne* weaves
a welcome new thread into the great tapestry of Southern
literature."
—**Michael Mejia**

"*Call Me Jeanne* is salty, funny, and wise. Like all good
comical memoirs, it's also, at heart, about matters of deep
emotional gravity. I love the book."
—**Michael Cunningham**, author, Yale writing professor

Acknowledgements

My thanks to the many who enlightened, encouraged and corrected me along the way.

Agnes Bass, decades long English teacher at Bacon County High School, started the story-telling ball rolling by announcing extra credit for an oral book report. She was speaking my language—no points off for spelling and punctuation. And, reporting three of Chaucer's Canterbury Tales garnered more credit. That sounded like a piece of cake. Little did I know the Tales were full of sex and naughty words but I was committed. I read every tale more than once to select the three I could clean up enough for a fifteen-year-old virgin to tell her male and female classmates. The embarrassing episode garnered an A+ for the semester and set me on the path of story-telling.

Fast forward sixty years: the Berry College English department professors welcomed a septuagenarian among the fresh-faced students filing in. The following two years are among my favorite memories and I wrote about the enriching experience.

The other reader/encouragers who went beyond expectation are legion: Michael Cunningham, Fran Stewart, James A. Autry, Carrie N. Baker, Ray Waters, Michael Mejia, Mindy Wilson, Jon Hershey, Stan Mitchell, and my family members. Jack Meyer, Diana Pascual, and Julie Blecha had unending patience to deal with my technical deficit and answered my pleas for help. In the early days, Sean Kilgore also bailed me out of many rabbit holes. These friends and many more kept me going with kind words of encouragement. I can't overstate the greatness of young friends as I celebrate 92 years of living.

Love,
Jeanne

Contents

Chapter One

Dixie Union Cocoon

Three mom and pop businesses and eleven houses comprised unincorporated Dixie Union, Georgia. Our family resided in three of those houses between 1934 and 1941. We were not evicted; we were upwardly mobile. My story began at a faded, whitewashed three-room house in the threadbare community bisected by U.S. Highway 1. Black Ford Model Ts and Model As rolled by at speeds up to thirty-five or even forty-five miles per hour. Astonishing!

Our shoebox size Philco was placed precariously on the window sill, so those outside on the porch could lean in close and hear over the static. Excited men shouted, stomped worn brogans, moonshine in their faded overalls, listened to a world heavy-weight boxing match on our tiny radio: Joe Louis and Max Schmeling, June 19, 1936.

Mother's request to keep the noise down was ignored. Gloria, my year-old sister, couldn't sleep, cried, and Daddy did not support Mother's request. I was angry with him; too young to grasp the significance of the boxing match to the listeners bereft of excitement, no radio of their own and no electricity. Those work weary men, farmers, struggling to feed families on the produce of over-stressed land, left quietly when the fight ended.

In retrospect, I wondered if they cheered for the American who was black or the German who was white. I put the

question to a ninety-something scholarly lawyer. His response
was, "Sorry to say it was the latter in North Georgia and
probably no different in South Georgia." A 2005 article in
The Guardian revealed the truth. Despite Louis's assertion he
was fighting for the "good old USA," white sports writers in
Jim Crow South "hankered for a German victory in the most
politically charged sporting bout in history." Hitler wanted to
exploit tall, blond Schmeling as an example of his master race.
Schmeling refused to become a Nazi and would not embrace
Hitler's agenda.

Dixie Union, a real place on the map, was an oddly named,
clannish settlement in the deep South, where Northerners
passed through on their way to Florida. Some locals saw the
KKK as respectable, impressed by the occasional line of hooded men making a show of their contribution at church. I never
witnessed this, but Mother, born in 1911, said it happened
when she was a child. My early views were shaped against this
backdrop, though thankfully, my parents were what we'd now
call "liberal."

Daddy did not ignore Mother's plea for quiet as the farmers
listened to the fight because he didn't care; rather, to give in to
a woman's request was unseemly, or worse, unmanly. This was
the rural south of the 1930s where unwritten rules were made
by men and followed by women and children who knew their
places. Daddy let the shouting continue.

An artist told me a first memory indicates a directional sign
guiding one's interest or career choices. Without conscious
awareness of such a destiny, I volunteered in political campaigns before I was old enough to vote. Women's rights were a
concern before I had a name for it!

Daddy's six-foot-two frame and Gary Cooper demeanor hid
the insecurity he masked with weekend closet drinking, a habit
he kept from us for years. He never raised his voice, used pro-
fanity, or missed a day of work. Like many men of his time, he
didn't acknowledge the weight women carried. He didn't help

with housework or childcare, except for occasionally taking the baby to see the garden, chickens, and cow—his sun-darkened arms gently cradling the child. We never doubted our parents' love. It wasn't spoken often, but shown through care and attention. From an early age, I saw men made the decisions, and women quietly followed, even in happy marriages.

Daddy's education started in 1917 when he was five, in the one-room Elizabeth Taylor Chapel next to the family farm. Cousins and neighbors studied together, first through eighth grades, with one teacher. They sat on hard pews, writing on slates, with gravestones visible through the windows. Upper classes were 25 miles away in Douglas, an all-day trip by mule and wagon. Boarding students worked to cover costs—Daddy milked cows and made butter, spending more time in the kitchen and barn than in class. Disillusioned after one semester, he returned to the farm. Self-taught in engine mechanics, this skill became his ticket out of Dixie Union when WWII loomed.

My relatives were colorful storytellers, vividly recounting events before I was birthed. Their stories let me witness the history of our forebears and the marriage of my parents, Wannie and Clifford, June 5, 1930. Her 1927 marriage to Robert Cornelius Barber ended tragically in less than a year. Barber was arrested for bigamy and desertion of his family in California; a fact he kept secret. Wannie Sweat, a married sixteen-year-old, in love, pregnant, was devastated as her husband was handcuffed and placed in the sheriff's car. She never saw or heard from Bob Barber again. Mother's only option was returning home, joining nine of her twelve siblings. Her family felt it was her fault for not knowing better while she silently suffered losing her husband and facing the future of her unborn child. Ironically, she was pressured by society to be engaged or married by the end of ninth grade, and she had reached that milestone.

Mother told me, "If you did not have a proposal of marriage at that point, people thought something was wrong with you."

She was pretty, popular, a free spirit, and Bob Barber quickly proposed, failing to mention his abandoned California family. Eight months after Barber's arrest, living in Waycross with her parents, Mother's baby boy was delivered and an annulment granted. The family thought it best to have the father's name on the birth certificate then file for annulment, preventing the disgrace of having a child out of wedlock.

Daddy and Mother, with one-year-old Bobby, moved to the Taylor farm with Daddy's three siblings. Mother said the Taylors were warm and welcoming to her and little Bobby. A year into this marriage, Wannie suffered another tragedy, a baby boy was stillborn. She never talked about it until I was an adult and I asked about her life's greatest disappointment. What did she wish for and never receive? I wanted to acknowledge the love and hard work of her eighty years. We were sitting in the gazebo at the Taylor farm, surrounded by fragrant, over-abundant flowers.

"It's the chicken manure," she answered when asked for her gardening secret.

Sipping a glass of chardonnay, teary-eyed, she told her story. "The baby looked perfect but never breathed. I don't think the doctor was competent; whiskey was on his breath."

Daddy built a tiny coffin. Wrapped in her handmade baby quilt, lovingly embroidered with lambs, the infant was buried with the ancestors at Elizabeth Chapel where wrought iron fencing enclosed ancient cedars and graves with dates from the 1800s.

"We could not afford a gravestone and planned to replace the wooden cross when things got better. The depression worsened, our move to Norfolk, followed by Jacksonville, resulted in lack of money for a permanent memorial. The wooden cross deteriorated."

She said the lack of visible acknowledgment of the baby's existence caused her great sorrow. Deep pain apparent more than eighty years after her baby's death.

"Mother, don't grieve," I said. "We will get your baby a marker."

Between Mother and Daddy's tombstones stands a little plaque, TAYLOR BABY BOY, 1931.

Daddy helped run the farm with his two brothers—James Lamar and Reddish Jackson (Jack)—and his father, James Madison Taylor, called Jimboy. He disliked farming and wanted a place of his own. He took a job that offered a rude cabin at Kirkland's turpentine distillery in Crawley, about eight miles south of the farm, where U.S. Highway 1 crosses the railroad tracks leading to Brunswick. A spur allowed rail cars to unhitch and load long leaf pine stumps bought from farmers clearing new ground. Hercules Powder Plant in Brunswick used the stumps for producing gun powder and dynamite. The distillery also bought the long leaf pine rosin dripped from chevron cuts into tin containers nailed to the tree. The rosin scooped from the small containers into buckets was transferred to barrels hauled to the facility on mule-driven flat sleds or wagons. Pickup trucks were rare and tractors almost unheard of.

Work was backbreaking; sticky tar coated everything. Only an iron wash pot filled with water, boiled over an outdoor fire, homemade lye soap, scrubbed on a washboard, removed tar covering the workmen's clothes. I don't know what Daddy's job was; it could not have been easy. Washing work clothes, cooking, and tending Bobby with sparse household goods, consumed Mother's days. She said her spirits remained high; this was the first time she and Daddy were independent, on their own. She was still a teenager, nineteen.

This first home of their own, little more than a shack without electricity or running water, was located at the distillery. In 1932 when my birth was imminent, little Bobby went to

Waycross with Mother's parents. Mrs. Kirkland, wife of the
distillery owner, insisted Mother move into her middle-class
home on U.S. Highway 1, across the highway from the three
laborer cabins, and remain for the requisite two weeks recovery
period. The doctor in attendance never filled out or recorded a
certificate of my birth. Mother said she was thrilled to hear my
first cry. She must have thought about the baby boy that never
made a sound.

Even during the Great Depression, Daddy managed to save
part of his small salary, determined to start his own business.
Less than a year after I was born, we moved to Dixie Union,
where Gloria was born in 1935 and my memories began with
the famous Joe Louis-Max Schmeling fight. Our tiny house
had a single light bulb hanging from the ceiling but no plumbing. Just off U.S. Highway 1, it had likely been a small store
before.

Hard times sparked the entrepreneurial spirit; Mother had
egg money. Daddy repaired cars, trucks, farm equipment, and
saved enough money to acquire Dixie Union's vacant Sinclair
service station in 1938. Friends with trucks helped move our
sparse possessions; no payment expected and none accepted.

From the three-room house, we moved about forty feet
south and across U.S. Highway 1 to a house attached to the
back of the Sinclair station. The house portion had a back
porch with a cold-water faucet, an outhouse, a fenced backyard, and a henhouse. A side porch swing where babies were
lulled to sleep commanded a view of vehicles on the highway.

Attached to the front of our house was a one-room forerunner of modern convenience stores. Candy, peanuts, ice-cream,
cold drinks, eggs, fan belts, oil, and automobile small parts
were among items available. The tempting sweets were for sale,
not for wide-eyed children occasionally given a silver bell (now
called kisses) or, for special events, a Choc-Cow: vanilla ice
cream coated in chocolate, mounted on a stick. Once, Bobby
talked me into "taking" five silver bells; he was the lookout.

The deal was I could keep two; he would get three. I didn't get caught. He stayed with us again while we had a house with more room.

Mother helped in the store when Daddy went to Waycross for automobile parts or was busy repairing vehicles in the garage a few yards to the right of the gas pumps. She could go from her kitchen through a connecting door into the store if a customer arrived. All the family shared in the work of the new enterprise. I gathered eggs and kept eyes on toddler Gloria.

The McCutchens from Northwest Georgia moved into our old house across the highway. Mr. McCutchen raved about a cottage industry where women made chenille bedspreads and robes in Calhoun and along Highway 41 between Atlanta and Chattanooga. He said our location was ideal with wealthy tourists passing by on U.S. Highway 1. Before long, we had a chenille machine, fabric, thread, and samples of bedspreads, robes, and bathmats to use as patterns. Gloria and I helped with simple tasks like twisting yarn for robe ties, and by age seven or eight, I could stamp designs on fabric.

This involved a finished item placed on the floor, bottom side up, covered with new cloth and a purple wax-coated bar rubbed over the cloth to transfer the pattern of stitches. Daddy strung clotheslines like gigantic wings on each side of the service station for displaying items sewn by Mother. The colorful peacock motif was the most popular and "Peacock Alley" originated along U.S. Highway 1; entrepreneurs from Dixie Union to Florida made chenille goods. This recently emerged technology spawned the carpet industry, created a number of millionaires in Northwest Georgia. Chenille bedspreads did not bring wealth to Dixie Union but they helped feed us.

Tourists on U.S. Highway 1 must have been amused to see free range children and chickens at a filling station with a side porch, a swing, flowery bedspreads, and an outhouse. We were allowed to play anywhere on our property, and a favorite activity was climbing pecan trees behind the service station/house.

The huge low-growing limbs, almost parallel to the ground, were perfect for reading and watching for a car with children aboard stopping for gas or a repair. With siblings as our lone playmates, we were quick to acknowledge a potential friend, if only briefly, while Daddy worked on a car.

Growing automobile production, the increase in traffic, and carnage on the roads attracted the attention of President Roosevelt and members of Congress. FDR saw the need for an interconnecting thoroughfare system. Disagreements arose over toll roads versus free, numbers needed, whether more accidents would result if food stands and taverns selling whiskey opened for travelers. The controversy around this subject was extensive and interesting. Some thought there might be as many as five east-west highways and seven to nine north-south routes.

Built in 1926, U.S. Highway 1 stretched 2,369 miles from Maine's Canadian border to Key West. It took one through the places we lived, where we children were born except Mac, who made his entrance in Norfolk, and where both sets of grandparents lived. In the1930s, the two-lane expressway carried ever-increasing traffic and was the site of frequent tragedy. Before the development of safety glass, passengers often bled to death from cuts inflicted by shards of broken windshields.

The Red Cross trained Daddy in basic first aid, provided a supply kit, and canvas stretcher. He was often first to be notified of accidents. December 1937, supper almost finished, a pickup truck screeched to a halt at our service station/house.

The driver yelled, "Clifford, get your stretcher, train hit a car at Crowley Distillery Crossing and it looks bad."

Daddy left immediately in his pickup truck with winch for pulling immobile vehicles. Catastrophes frequently occurred at this poorly marked crossing where an unlighted sign on a pole with the familiar "RR-X" warned the driver, no markings or reflectors on the pavement. Few telephones existed and Daddy was often the only contact during a painful wait as someone drove to find a doctor or an ambulance. He was a gentle man, avoided confrontation. I am sorry I never asked him how he felt about the carnage he saw at the sight of wrecks along his stretch of U.S. Highway 1. He didn't talk about the wrecks beyond a brief account of the facts. After a couple of hours he returned, towing a Packard coupe with the front smashed at an angle. We rushed out to look at the car, to hear what happened.

"They were dead when I got there, a young couple from New York apparently on their honeymoon. All I could do was wait while someone drove to town to send the ambulance."

"Just Married" in white paint covered the rear window, and I saw one blood-spattered, fur-trimmed, ankle high black boot on the floor of the passenger side. It was the most beautiful shoe I had ever seen. I wanted to pick it up but Daddy said leave it alone. Years later, I would understand he had a sense of privacy, or even a sacredness, about things to be left untouched and accounts unsaid. In Dixie Union, adults wore brogans, Oxfords, or pumps. Children went barefoot except in cold weather. No one we knew owned such a beautiful boot. This wreck is etched in memory due to the circumstances: a new-ly-wed couple dying so young, and the sadness of one bloody shoe in the bloody car.

Early I learned the meaning of death. Details were ex-changed between adults, children listening. I watched my grandfather build a pine box for the burial of an elderly woman who lived alone in the Taylor farm community. With no family to care for her, a wake was held with neighbors sitting up all night in my grandparent's parlor. All the funerals of my early years were conducted at Elizabeth Chapel— the religious, social, and educational center of the community.

We are Scots-Irish descendants living with the belief a clan takes care of its own. I witnessed hogs killed with a well-placed sledge hammer to the skull, a steer taken to the slaughter house, or a chicken's neck wrung for Sunday dinner. These tasks were part of everyday events on a farm; no feeling of sadness.

The death of the young couple was different. Tragic. My parents' grim faces, as Daddy recounted the death, made me cry for people I didn't know. As Mother reached her comforting arms to pull us close, I thought about the parents and relatives far away and how I would hate to die alone in a strange place.

Other wrecks occurred along the highway, other deaths, but none affected me like this one. A sadness emerges when I see a fashionably dressed woman's fur-trimmed boot, back in style eighty years later.

We met tourists heading south from places as distant as Canada. Daddy's reputation as an excellent mechanic spread among New Yorkers and others who stopped to have a car checked or repaired before the last leg of their trip. After weeks or months in Florida, some regulars stopped to buy gas and visit as they returned north. We were treated to wondrous sights: snow on running boards of southbound cars, pets fed from silver bowls, mouths wiped with cloth napkins. We grew up with yard dogs and barn cats that lived on table scraps, mouths never wiped with anything.

When she saw our chickens, one woman asked to buy four eggs. From a small sewing basket, she retrieved tiny scissors with a gold-colored handle shaped like a bird and proceeded to make a hole in the eggs, handing one to each member of her party. Watching four adults sucking a raw egg from its shell nearly made me gag.

We played around the service station, and while Daddy often reminded us to watch for cars, I don't remember being told to stay in the backyard or on the porch. In the 1930s, cars were fewer, slower, and accidents were more of a curiosity. I only had one minor injury playing out front.

The tall gas pumps with long hoses from the glass tanks made perfect swings for a small child. One day, while swinging, the heavy metal nozzle fell and hit my head, leaving a scar. As usual, no doctor was called—just soap, water, and a drop of kerosene to clean it. After that, the gas hose swing was off-limits.

On rare occasions, we received gifts from travelers who from previous visits became friends. The truth is they probably felt sorry for a gaggle of sweet little barefoot kids whose "park" was the dirt yard around the service station or the fenced area shared with chickens. They apologized as they offered slightly worn children's clothing.

"My friend whose children have outgrown these clothes would appreciate it if your children or someone you know can use them. It's a favor to her if you can make use of items they no longer need."

We were thrilled. We could barely wait for the car to leave before we tried on and claimed whatever fit. We had no idea we were poor, and these were rich people's castoffs. It was like hand-me-downs from cousins, only better; these outfits and shoes were nicer, not already half worn-out.

A traveling family with a son my age asked to take pictures of me. While the woman chatted with Mother, we were sent outside to play. They left, promising to send a snapshot. Weeks later, a letter arrived on New York Yacht Club stationery with the photo. I barely glanced at it—me, barefoot in a dirty dress, standing next to the boy in a crisp white suit. Years later, Mother told me the woman had asked to take me to live with their family in New York.

She said "You have so many children (four, and another was on the way) and I can have no more, only our little boy."

They offered a fine school, the advantages of a city, nice friends, a long visit every winter en route to Florida. Also, Mother's expenses paid to visit any time, a safe offer to a woman who traveled no more than thirty miles from her birthplace.

Mother told the woman, "I would not take a million dollars for one of my little ones, or give a nickel for another one after this next birth."

Years later, I asked Mother about this request, whether people actually gave away their offspring if they could not afford to feed and clothe them.

Mother said, "I hated to disappoint the woman from New York but there was no way I could give up one of you children."

She said she heard of desperately poor people surrendering a child to someone to raise. "I don't personally know anyone who gave away a child and I'm not sure it ever happened. It could be hearsay, and I can't imagine how hungry or sick your children would be before you made that choice." Mother said she would go hungry and barefoot if that was the only way to have food and clothing for her babies. I never doubted the veracity of her statement. Always gentle with us, she was a lioness if necessary.

Beyond the fenced back yard of the Sinclair building was a garden and a milk cow. Vegetables frequently accepted instead of cash for repairs on a local car or truck. I asked Mother how they managed during the Depression.

"We ate well because of bartering—milk, eggs, chickens, and sometimes your daddy's work traded for a pig to slaughter; we had cash only for essentials."

Our family kept growing; James and Jerry were born during our years at the Sinclair station. Like all of Mother's babies, we were born at home with the aid of a country physician. I had no idea how babies were conceived, or how they got here. James miraculously appeared while I was sent out to play and, eighteen months later, Jerry arrived while I was at school. He was in Mother's arms when I came home for lunch.

Mother often recalled October 30, 1938, when Jerry was just six days old. Confined to bed after giving birth, she listened to *War of the Worlds* on the radio, unaware it was fiction. Panic swept the nation as listeners believed it was a real invasion. Mother said it was the biggest scare of her life. With four young children and a newborn, and Daddy away, she got on her feet, desperate to figure out what to take and where to go.

Her cousin, Flora Jordan Sharp, there to help with the baby, was also distraught over the radio announcement until Daddy arrived and said it was a fictional story. Everyone settled down and Mother got back to bedrest with her baby. Our world was small. The idea of running away from an invasion or anything else was unthinkable.

I often rang the bell that called students to Dixie Union School, which had four rooms: one for first and second grades, another for third and fourth, and two more for fifth and sixth. With outhouses and a hand pump for water, it was a simple setup. I finished my first-grade work early and moved on to the next level. Miss Eunice Lee, my teacher, wisely had me tutor struggling first graders. I loved it. When a little girl asked to "borry yore yeller crayoller," I made her repeat it until she got it right before handing her my crayon. The third and fourth grade teacher, Miss Henderson, did the same when I completed both years' work early, having me help other students again.

Most students lived on farms outside the immediate community, their families struggled to survive. Except for seeing poorly dressed farm children at school with syrup buckets containing lunch, sometimes only biscuits, I knew little about them or their home lives. The only other students living in Dixie Union, besides my siblings and me, were Nell Lott and our paper delivery boy, Jack Roland. They rode a bus to high school. Nell's parents owned a tourist court with two overnight rental cabins, each with a bedroom and bath. Travelers had few choices in the years before motels became the norm along the highways. I liked to help Mrs. Lott clean the rooms; she once gave me a little red knit hat some girl left behind. I remember it as a fabulous find.

I realized we had more money than our farmer neighbors when, at Christmas, my parents bought enough apples and oranges for every student—about 100—to have one of each. The children saved their fruit to share at home, treating it like a treasure. When the government truck arrived with large brown bags of butter, canned milk, cheese, beans, and other staples, many families relied on that food to get through the Depression. Without it, they would have suffered greatly.

School nurses brought vaccines, others arrived with bars of pink soap, tooth brushes, and Ipana toothpaste. These government-sponsored efforts were tremendously helpful to a struggling South and FDR was revered. "Thank God and FDR" was sometimes heard for something positive like sustenance or the Rural Electric Association (REA) of 1936, bringing electricity to the farms. Prior to this act only ten percent of southern farms had electricity. I was four when I watched Daddy and Uncle Lamar string a wire to the center of a room, add a fixture to hold a light bulb, pull the attached chain and, like a miracle, there was light. My favorite chore, carefully washing the smoke from the glass lamp chimneys, suddenly disappeared.

Hobos walked south along the highway, most stopped, looked for food, were never turned away. They always asked if there was some work they could do for a meal. Mother let them rake leaves, sweep the porch, or any job she could come up with.

She said, "It lets them keep their dignity if they feel it is earned; not just a handout." Often, she gave them a biscuit with bacon or ham to take along for the road.

One day, a burgundy automobile—rare among the usual black ones—pulled into the garage with engine trouble. It had white sidewall tires and a rumble seat. Daddy said it was a Dodge. Two young men got out and asked how much the repair would cost. Out of money and unable to drive it safely, they offered to exchange it for cash to buy bus tickets and food for their trip back to New York. They had been living off canned goods and sleeping in the car, and saving what little they had for gas until the engine gave out near Dixie Union.

Daddy agreed to the bargain, drove the men to Waycross, bought bus tickets, and gave them cash for food on their long journey. Meanwhile, our excitement over the auto was short-lived. Daddy said the parts were expensive and we needed resources more than another vehicle; he repaired and sold it. Until a buyer came along, Daddy drove it and we little passengers would head for the rumble seat. We were adamant about who had ridden there last, whose turn it was, and how many of us could squeeze in; (three, if two were tiny). Our parents did not discuss finances in our presence but concern for the future, for necessities, was ever present.

On a cold, windy day in 1939, I saw my mother cry for the first time. Daddy had gone to start a neighbor's car while Mother bathed and dressed us for a Sunday visit to her parents in Waycross—a quick and simple task in today's world—but it required water from a faucet on the back porch to fill the zinc washtub, heated on the kerosene cook stove and a fire built in the fireplace. Four children were bathed near the fire to keep warm in our drafty house.

Our clothing was homemade or hand-me-downs divided into categories: good, school, and play. Rarely was there more than one outfit acceptable to put on for an outing. Mother dressed the baby last; the rest of us, clean and dressed, huddled near the fire when a sudden chimney downdraft blew soot into the room, landing on our clean skin and our best outfits. A look of disbelief, then tears rolled down Mother's cheeks as she sat immobile, black spotted baby Jerry in her lap. Even at an early age I knew her work was demanding and the situation almost too much for a hardworking mother to bear. The spectacle of four children and their mother covered in spots of black soot, dotting the floor, the chairs, and the bed–there was always a bed in every room but the kitchen–might elicit gales of laughter today, but in 1938 life was serious business. I don't know if Mother attempted to make us presentable or if the trip was aborted. I only remember her sad face and being frightened because she was always happy and I had never seen her cry.

Most memories are happy ones—Mother cooking, music always playing on the radio, holding a small child, and dancing around the kitchen. She taught all of us how to dance, including the Jitterbug, and she stressed the importance of proper grammar. No baby talk, and definitely no slang, was allowed. I don't know how Mother acquired aspirational thinking but it was always there with her sense of trying to do better and expecting the same of her children.

Movies arrived in Dixie Union marking a new high in entertainment. A tent was set up and backless wooden benches placed under the cool long leaf pines, shiny brown pine needles for a floor and a 5-cent admission for children. In the semi-darkness, grainy images with split second pauses between each frame flickered across the screen and I fell in love with Gene Autry. I ran home, a few yards away, with my eyes blinking like the movie projector.

Mother said, "Stop that blinking or you won't see another movie in a tent."

I walked around, held my eyes open zombie-like and fantasized about marrying Gene. In my day-dreaming we rode down the center of U.S. Highway 1. He in his beautiful cowboy outfit, white from boots to ten-gallon-hat. I sat behind him, naked, my arms around his middle. Amazing thoughts for a five or six-year-old who knew nothing about sex, public nakedness, or Lady Godiva. I simply knew Gene was the most gorgeous man I had ever seen and I wanted him to sing to me, to make me part of his life. This movie awakened me to a world beyond Dixie Union, bookended by Alma, six miles north and Waycross ten miles south.

While we lived in Dixie Union, I saw three movies at a theater in Waycross: Steamboat 'Round the Bend with Will Rogers, 1936; Snow White, 1938; and Wizard of Oz, 1939. A movie in a real theater was a rare treat. I disliked the Steamboat one (Mother liked it) but the other two mesmerized me. I named my Christmas doll Judy Garland and again had the idea we had money because of that pretty doll, the finest present I'd ever received.

Interaction was rare other than with a few tourists, family, and neighbors trying to survive. As meager as life was for us, it was worse for the black families scattered about the countryside. Before I began my formal education, I rode with Mother to Waycross and we passed a modest unpainted church where black children of various ages were playing in the yard. I asked why they were not in school.

"That *is* their school," she said.

I thought, "It must be awfully cold in winter because there is no glass in the windows." Those embers of sympathy remained with me.

I went with Daddy to a Negro woman's cabin, a pile of dirty clothes tied in a bed sheet on the back seat of our car. There must have been a new baby in our house because that's the only time we could afford help. We returned a few days later to pick up clean, starched, ironed, and folded clothes and linens. I watched Daddy count out three dollars for all that work. The woman appeared grateful. The average annual wage in the 1930s was $1,650. A pound of hamburger meat was ten cents; three dollars bought a week's groceries. Black people near Dixie Union were quiet, stayed to themselves, and caused no trouble. The white people, if they mentioned the blacks, would generally refer to them as hard-working humble folks that knew their place. Later, I realized that meant subservience, little freedom, and probably fear of the KKK.

I learned early about a secret hate group on a visit to the home of Dave Bennett, a friend of my parents. On the mantel were statues of three scary white-robed figures—large, medium, and small. Looking at them gave me a bad feeling and on the way home I asked Mother why were ghosts on the mantel.

She said, "Those are Klan figures representing a group, usually community leaders, organized to keep law and order, to protect women and children. Many are getting out of hand and now lots of people don't like what they do."

She said she was surprised to see Dave was a member. It was a long time before I realized the Klan was a way white men controlled black males in the guise of protecting women.

During a childhood visit to the farm, I overheard men telling my grandfather a disturbing story—they didn't know I was nearby. They laughed about wrapping a man in a bedsheet and tormenting him with a buggy whip. I was shocked when my gentle granddaddy chuckled. Though he wasn't part of any hateful group, he said nothing to condemn the cruelty. Knowing the pain a buggy whip could inflict, I imagined the terror of being helpless and beaten. I never spoke of it, but I knew something was deeply wrong.

Life in Dixie Union during the thirties was quiet, and while I'm sure there was abuse toward the Black community, I never heard about it. What I did see was the cruelty white women faced, beaten by their husbands. Sometimes, a woman with a black eye or bruises stayed with us until her husband sobered up. Mother tried to shield us with excuses like "falling down the steps," but I never believed her. One man, Hamp Tanner, stands out—his wife came more than once, clearly abused. These women were isolated on farms, with no car or phone, relying on neighbors to escape. They always went back for their children. Sometimes, even their own parents turned them away, saying, "You made your bed; now sleep in it." No one ever called the law. Women were almost entirely subservient, and mothers rarely defended their daughters, likely out of fear.

Our father was a gentle man who treated us well and did not demand subservience. He was often called on to discipline us; the boys got the worst of it, sometimes the belt would come off. Mother would send a perpetrator of misbehavior for her hairbrush, or a "keen little switch" to sting the legs. She was not afraid to make decisions and occasionally stretch the boundaries, unlike the many women who lived in fear of their husbands.

Strange are the little events I recall after nine decades. One afternoon, Daddy went to Waycross for auto parts. Mother was in charge of the Sinclair station, talking with her cousin, Flora Sharp, when a tobacco salesman stopped by with cigarette samples to give to customers. The salesman left and the adventurous women decided to try a sample. The minute Mother put it between her lips, before she could strike the match, Gloria and I simultaneously let out a loud cry. Mother jerked the white stick away.

"What on Earth is wrong?" she asked.

"Don't smoke," we said.

I never saw another one in her hand and I have no idea why we were upset at that sight.

Mother and Daddy rarely went out, but sometimes they visited the Gingham Inn, a juke joint owned by Woodrow and Blanche Carter, located between Dixie Union and Waycross on U.S. Highway 1. Sometimes they took us kids along. The Carters lived in a house attached to the restaurant, where the kitchen opened onto the dance floor. Wooden booths lined the walls, and red and white gingham cloths covered the simple, homemade tables.

We would play in the kitchen with the Carter girls and watch the dancers through the open door. I was happy to see my parents having fun, a rare sight because they worked morning to night at the service station, house, garden, and looking after children.

Gloria and I had curly hair, and for special occasions, Mother would tear strips of fabric from her ragbag, wrap our wet hair around them, and tie them into knots. Once dry, the result was more Shirley Temple curls than frizz. I don't know how she found the time, but she was determined to make us look as polished as possible with our old shoes, rag curls, and Octagon soap.

Daddy's service station became profitable, and we moved into a better house directly across the highway, back to the west side of U.S. Highway 1. A white picket fence enclosed the front yard, indoor plumbing, four bedrooms, and a porch spanned the front. It was the last house we would occupy in Dixie Union and the first one that didn't have the usual bed in the living room. In addition to the service station and chenille bedspreads, no entrepreneurial opportunity was wasted. One of the four bedrooms was furnished nicely and a cardboard sign advertised a room for rent to the traveling public: twenty-five cents for the room, ten cents for breakfast. The young son of the woman who occasionally did our washing and ironing was hired for ten cents to stand near the highway in late afternoon, holding a sign advertising the room.

This house and this venture were short-lived due to rapidly escalating military events in 1930s Europe. Grownups clustered around radios, listened to the latest news of events as Hitler began his devastation of the countries bordering Germany. Discussion was muted around children, signaling something bad happening in a strange, faraway country, was worrying our parents.

In the spring and summer of 1941, green military trucks rumbled along U.S. Highway 1, with rolled up canvas sides and benches carrying smiling young men tossing notes with addresses, calling out "write me" to girls and women, including my teachers, who waved and blew kisses. I joined the excitement, waving and smiling. I did not comprehend the gravity behind the bravado of the young men in the army trucks. We were not at war, but concern was evident in the expressions of the adults.

Word spread, told of jobs available in military installations, manufacturing plants, and shipyards, places far from the sleepy hamlet we knew. News of work was a godsend for those struggling to survive the Great Depression without hope of a job. The lure of a paycheck was not ignored.

Daddy learned of available work for engine mechanics at the Norfolk, Virginia, Naval Air Station. He drove there in late spring of 1941, applied for work, and was immediately hired to test engines in small planes destined to help our European Allies. Perhaps he realized with the prospect of war and the knowledge gas would be rationed, his gas station would be hard-pressed to remain successful. He returned to Dixie Union with the news he was hired, beginning at once.

Military families flooded into Norfolk, created a housing shortage and Daddy put his name on a waiting list for a house to rent. He lived in a boarding house, homesick, and longed to have us with him. He hoped for a rental house. Except for a short stint in boarding school, Daddy lived his entire life with his parents, and later with Mother, never alone.

With news of Daddy's job, a flurry of activity consumed us. We closed the service station, packed furniture and household goods and moved to the Taylor farm where we waited for a house. Summer ended and Gloria and I enrolled in Alma public schools while Bobby moved to our Waycross grandparents' home and enrolled in Wacona School. We hated to see Daddy leave us for a distant, unfamiliar place, but Mother, Gloria, James, Jerry, and I loved living with our grandparents.

Dixie Union rapidly became a ghost-community as job seekers and their families found work, many going to the Brunswick shipyard.

"Clifford," Mother said. "We'll never get the money owed for the work you've done on credit all these years." Mother was prescient.

People scattered in all directions, many never to return to dirt poor farms and hard scrabble businesses in Dixie Union.

With the bombing of Pearl Harbor on December 7, 1941, thoughts of short-term jobs and temporary moves vanished. We would never return to our little community and simple way of life among people who knew us from the time we were born.

We waited six months at the Taylor farm before traveling up U.S. Highway 1 to Virginia. Four children, two parents—plus whatever we could pack into the car—left our familiar Taylor farm. Bobby stayed behind with the Sweat grandparents until we were settled. We joined the job-seeker diaspora. World War II was a huge mixer of people and cultures from every corner of the United States. We were destined to become tiny fish in the largest pond we had ever seen.

Chapter Two

Living in the Bullseye

WWII, December 7, 1941, FDR's "Day that lives in infamy," changed millions of lives overnight including ours. In Norfolk work increased for civil service personnel as troops were reassigned to distant locations, ships sailed east from Chesapeake Bay, trains loaded with military personnel and supplies rolled to the west coast. Daddy checked engines installed in planes destined for America's Allies resulting from President Roosevelt's HR1776 Lend Lease Bill.

A rental house became available and Daddy headed south to gather his family. He arrived in Alma on Christmas Day, loudly sounded his car's horn at the left turn from U.S. Highway 1 onto the dirt lane that led to the farm house. Never away from us before, we swarmed him like Granddaddy's bees crawling over the hive. No time to waste; Daddy must return to work as quickly as possible. With urgency the car was loaded.

Daddy said, "Bring what you need because there is a shortage of everything in Norfolk."

The car was packed with clothes, linens, household items, the chenille machine, and non-perishable food, leaving barely enough room for two adults and four kids—Gloria, James, Jerry, and me, aged two to nine. Tears streaked our faces as we left our grandparents, waving from their porch until we crested the hill. The sadness of leaving was softened by the excitement of reuniting with Daddy for a new adventure. Our crowded car reminded me of the Gypsies along U.S. Highway 1, their wagons loaded with pots and pans clattering as mules swayed under the weight.

New Year's Day, 1942, we arrived at a Norfolk motel, bitter wind pushing us inside where we would stay four days. Two well-worn motel rooms with kitchenette, heated by a radiator into which quarters were constantly fed, produced a slight degree of warmth. The two-burner cook stove functioned when quarters were inserted. Weary from the drive we shivered in barely warm rooms; we didn't resist early bedtime. We awoke to unnatural brightness, thrilled to see snow blanketed everything as we slept. After a quick breakfast we donned our heaviest clothing and discovered the door was frozen shut. Before Daddy could leave for work, Mother heated two kettles of water to pour around the door to force it open. Once freed from our cramped, temporary dwelling we rushed out to play in the beautiful white fluffy snowscape.

We were in a flat parking lot with little chance of danger but mother insisted we hold hands. When fingers and toes became numb, reluctantly we went inside, put our wet clothes on the creaking, ill-working radiator. Week's end came and we were excited to move into our two-story house, half of a duplex, overlooking Chesapeake Bay between Norfolk and Virginia Beach.

The front door opened into a small living room, then a dining table with four chairs, kitchen, one bedroom, and a bathroom. Two bedrooms filled the upstairs. Mother fed us before Daddy arrived from work around 5:30 p.m. Four chairs were no problem; we ate in shifts most of the time. A two-lane highway and a few low dunes separated the house from the Chesapeake Bay and we were anxious for the cold wind to subside and spring temperatures arrive.

Our migration marked the beginning of the end of our family's personal Great Depression and opened a new world where purchases were made with money from something called a paycheck. We were part of a diaspora from the rural south to wherever jobs existed.

Gloria and I enrolled in Princess Ann School; James and Jerry too young for first grade and there were no kindergartens. Bobby, stayed with the Sweat grandparents, joining us during summer break. We missed visits to grandparents; even telephoning was not an option as newcomers were put on a phone wait list. We were in Norfolk eleven months and never reached the top of the list.

The first evening in the duplex we were startled by loud banging on the door at 5 p.m., accompanied by shouts of "Douse the lights." This was our introduction to the block's no nonsense air raid warden. Light fades early that far north and Mother struggled to get everyone fed, bathed, and in pajamas before the warden hit the door with his heavy flashlight, no excuses allowed. All windows had blackout curtains; a sliver of candle light was unacceptable. The two-lane road from Virginia Beach, a few miles east of our house, passed Norfolk Naval Air Station and the town of Norfolk to the west. The road—heavily traveled by military vehicles with hooded lights—was the only obstacle between us and the grey-green water of Chesapeake Bay. The inlet was a gentle, welcoming body of water where small waves rolled onto the beach with a whisper, a swooshing ocean lullaby.

We learned the danger of German U-boats slipping into the bay and the need for total darkness along the shoreline. With little to do after twilight, we made an exciting discovery. Lying on an upstairs bed, we watched through the windows and counted the silhouettes of blacked-out ships forming convoys. These ships, loaded with planes, tanks, and Jeeps, crept eastward toward the Atlantic. By morning, the calm water gave no hint of the night's activity. We quickly understood why no light could escape from houses along the estuary, unaware we were just miles from a key target for Germany.

Spring-warmed sand and air turned the beach into our favorite playground, but we were not allowed to get in the water
without an adult present. Mother was sure we would drown.
We watched coastal birds dive into shallow water and fly up
with something in their beaks.

"Look, Gloria! The seagulls are dropping something on the
concrete. Oh, wow."

"It's a clam, a real clam. I've seen a picture of one and I think
people eat them. That bird likes it and I bet Mother could cook
them."

Gloria's reply of "Yuck! They look slimy," didn't deter us.

We dumped the sand from our bucket and watched the
the large gray and white birds while we figured out how to
catch the released mollusks. Once they shattered, they became
coated with sand. The birds scooped them from shallow water
as waves receded, flew high over an old concrete walk, and
released their catch. The clam shells broke on contact with the
concrete and the birds swooped down to eat the contents. Our
pail strategically placed, we stood on either side, ready to run
in the direction a bird headed. We caught a few clams with
our basket and some in our bare hands then scurried across
the road to show Mother. With food rationed and meat often
non-existent, a pile of clams was a welcome gift.

Mother exclaimed, "You girls are great. No more meatless
suppers with a bay full of clams at our front door. Without
our garden, chickens and cow, it's hard to make a decent meal.
Food stamps help but the stores don't have much to offer."

We smiled as she later told Daddy, "The girls are responsible
for this tasty seafood dinner."

Clams provided a renewed since of pride in contributing
something of value. My old jobs of gathering eggs, or shelling
peas, no longer existed. I knew Mother's work never ended and
I believed my job was helping her.

Bobby, thirteen, spent the summer racing seagulls and
catching clams with ease. But his most exciting find wasn't a

clam. One day, as the waves receded, he pulled a half-buried submariner's cap from the sand, marked with a swastika. Radio reports had warned of German U-boats in the Bay and along the Atlantic shore. Not long after Bobby's discovery, a newspaper reported that two German submariners had been captured in Norfolk, with movie ticket stubs from Granby Theater in their pockets. They had likely come ashore at our beach during the night, avoiding detection from the nearby military installation, while we played, unaware of the danger.

Norfolk Naval Air Station was a critical facility sending defense materiel to the European Allies. I don't know its 1942 size when we were there but a news report dated 2017 indicated it is the largest naval installation ever built. I was a carefree child with no idea we lived and played near one of the largest targets in the world. No one could enter the base without special passes; and to keep Mother from undue worry, Daddy never mentioned the dangers of his work place. We were living, working, and playing in the bullseye. The war could have gone very differently had FDR not instigated and signed the Lend Lease Bill, providing aid to European Allies. Hitler was bombing London mercilessly as Prime Minister Winston Churchill begged the U.S. for help. In Eric Larson's book, "The Splendid and the Vile," a conversation in which Randolph Churchill told his father there was no way England could survive but the Prime Minister insisted they would prevail. When pressed for how that could happen, Churchill said, "I'm going to drag the United States in." That explains the Lend Lease bill passed by Congress and the convoys of ships stealthily slipping out of Chesapeake Bay under cover of darkness, carrying planes with engines tested by Daddy. I have a valuable artifact from the period, related to Churchill's statement.

A treasure given to me by Christie McWhorter in 1985, one of five pens of intrinsic value used by President Roosevelt in signing H.R. 1776, March 11, 1941. A letter from the Whitehouse written to Senator Walter F. George accompanied the pen which marked a crucial event in world history. Churchill called it "The most unsordid act in the history of any nation." Stalin said this act alone allowed the Allies to survive. It explained why Daddy was hired six months before the Japanese attacked the United States at Pearl Harbor and we entered the war.

Reminders of war engulfed our lives. Mundane purchases required more than stamps for food, shoes, gas, tires, and other necessities. To purchase canned goods, empty cans were returned: washed, both ends cut off with a manual can opener and flattened. A new tube of toothpaste—before plastic—required an empty metal tube in exchange. Foil packaging of chewing gum, cigarettes and other items was saved, rolled into a ball, turned in when it was a few inches in circumference.

One of my tasks was mixing oleomargarine into something passing for butter. A pound block of white lard-like material accompanied by a small packet of dark orange powder required integrating. With a potato masher and lots of patience, a passable degree of uniformity resulted; no one complained about a few streaks of orange. After tiresome mixing, the glob was shaped into a lopsided rectangle tasting nothing like real butter but, at least, it lubricated toast. Mother was dismayed to learn boxes of grits were not a staple at grocery stores, only bland hominy. She notified acquaintances coming to Norfolk to bring the coarsely ground grain. Breakfast with Mother was a big meal and buttered grits a staple. No one left for school or work without eating.

Wartime events impacted people we knew. Daddy's friend, Mr. Miller, of German heritage, lost his job as a drawbridge operator on a creek leading to Chesapeake Bay. After decades of service, he was devastated, labeled a "potential Nazi sympathizer" with no hope of finding new work. There was no support for people like him, just as there was none for the Japanese Americans interned on the West Coast.

My classmate Margaret lived nearby, and we often sat on the beach watching ships. Once, we searched the horizon for the oil tanker carrying her father. A wisp of black smoke appeared in the distance—his ship had been hit by a torpedo but managed to limp home. Nothing was reported in the paper. A few months later, Margaret tragically died when she ran behind the school bus to cross the street. A military ambulance, hidden from her view by the bus, hit her as we watched in shock from the windows. There were no grief counselors back then, and little was said about this or other tragedies.

After Bobby arrived for the summer, and with a baby due in June—though pregnancy was never mentioned—we found a larger house on Lake Joyce, a small private fishing lake with two houses; one became ours, the other occupied by the Dowdy family. It was on the same highway as the duplex, a couple of miles nearer Norfolk's prime target and Daddy's work at NAS. The exciting news was the house came with a small rowboat and a lake full of fish, a welcome change from clams. Fish fries prevented the boredom of meatless meals and Bobby liked nothing better than fishing. He and a friend caught fifty-two breams in one day. We shared them with the Dowdy's who generously gave us a rabbit when we became their neighbor. They grew rabbits in cages and they had a victory garden which we helped tend in exchange for surplus vegetables. We weren't in one place long enough to plant a garden of our own.

Teenage Angie Dowdy cared for the rabbits and she gave me my first inadequate lesson about sex. We observed one bunny as it climbed on the back of another which I interpreted as being mean, hurting the one on the bottom. After a short time, Angie reached in the pen, removed the bottom hare, turned it over to reveal pink skin, white fur carefully parted by "the boy rabbit so he could put his thing in and later there would be baby rabbits coming out of the same place."

A kind and generous spirit permeated the country with much sharing of whatever one had. It was already a common practice for us; farmers traditionally shared surplus crops. Gasoline was an ever-present concern but carpooling to work, grocery stores, and shopping (a rare occurrence), stretched precious gas coupons to the maximum.

A Sunday visit to others from South Georgia, many who stayed with us while finding work and a place to live, was a treat only possible when there was an extra gallon of gas. Our baby brother was born June 19, weighing eleven pounds, twelve ounces, and named Joseph McArthur for his grandfather, Joseph Atwell Sweat, and General Douglas McArthur, the reigning military hero of 1942. We children didn't know a birth was eminent, only that mother was lying down because she was tired. To cheer her up we brought to her room a large turtle we saw sunning on a log beside Lake Joyce. It got loose and crawled out of reach under her bed just as a strange man arrived carrying a black leather case. We were told by Aunt Lola to "quickly go outside and play," the same instructions we heard before the births of James and Jerry. When we were allowed back inside, the doctor said, "That's the first baby I ever delivered with a turtle watching."

In 1942, home births were common natural births, assisted by a doctor or midwife, no anesthesia, female relatives usually the only helpers. Playing near, we heard no scream from our small mother, no outcry as Mac, almost twelve pounds, entered our world. I truly don't know how she did it, unless, through sheer force of will, she was determined not to frighten her children playing outside. This was the sixth home delivery for her; seven if you count the stillbirth of 1931.

Mother's stoicism as she endured unimaginable pain was on my mind decades later in Atlanta as I experienced the rigors of natural childbirth. In 1964 as I delivered a baby weighing less than eight pounds surrounded by a doctor, two nurses, and an anesthesiologist ("just in case," the doctor said), I literally thought I might die, but I remembered the 1942 silence of Mother each time I wanted to scream. My eyes locked onto a large clock on the wall beyond my bent knees. It seemed stuck on each unending minute. A small tray positioned near my head held a filled hypodermic needle, pointed out by Dr. Smith.

He said, "There is no point in suffering needlessly. If the pain is too intense, we can end it in seconds," as he nodded toward the needle on the tray.

That strengthened my resolve to not have my baby drugged. I set goals of getting through five minutes, then another five, then another. Next followed goals of one minute, then another as I could barely suppress the need to scream or hit someone or something.

"Push, push," and with what felt like my last vestige of energy, the last deep breath, a lusty cry filled that cold, sterile setting. With tears streaming, "Is it a girl or a boy?" I asked.

"A girl, a perfect baby girl," the nurse said as she laid a swaddled, tiny human across my chest.

"Her daddy will be so happy," I loudly proclaimed.

"Well, you sound pretty excited yourself," the doctor said.

"I am, I am. We already have a son, now this is perfect."

With that, Carol was whisked away to the nursery where Al could see her through a glass wall. He waited more than an hour before I was removed to a room he would be allowed to enter. It was many hours after birth when Carol was brought to me with the explanation a stillbirth had occurred and the distraught family needed the available personnel. By that time, visitors were in the hallway and Carol would have to wait until they all left. It was four hours later that she was brought to my room after I announced I would get out of bed and go to the nursery to get her.

I am glad mothers and fathers of today can celebrate and strengthen each other in kinder, gentler ways and with support for many methods of childbirth. I can hardly believe Mother's stoicism delivering a baby weighing nearly twelve pounds. This glimpse at childbirth's change in two decades showed improvements, though not nearly enough, and an evolving change benefitting parents and child continued.

Mother's delivery was followed by two weeks bed rest. Daddy's brother, Lamar, and his wife, Lola, stayed with us waiting for a place to rent when Mac was born. Lamar operated a dredge boat deepening channels at Little Creek Naval Base. Aunt Lola looked after Mother and little Mac and did the cooking. She made a pie, cooled on the wide sill of an open window without screens, something we never did in Dixie Union because of ever present houseflies. It was like a picture in a magazine. That vivid image strengthened my nascent interest in homemaking as a "career."

Uncle Lamar didn't give details about his work and only in researching this period did I learn dredging was critical preparation for training troops for the D-Day invasion planned for Normandy. He was excavating channels through a former bean field to the Chesapeake Bay. Armed forces practiced exiting landing craft into the channels he dug and slogged their way onto the Chesapeake beach similar to the geography of Normandy, France, where 163,000 U.S. and Allied soldiers would make up the largest land, sea, and air operation ever undertaken. Lamar's previous work involved dredging the Tamiami Trail through the Florida Everglades.

Mother sat in bed most evenings, Mac in her lap nursing. Gloria, James, Jerry, and I wreathed her as she read from Mother Goose. The stories were familiar but I loved hearing her read them again. She was either pregnant or breast feeding a baby for more than seventeen years, yet managed to make time for all her children. Labor-saving devices did not exist in her world.

Our parents were homesick; never separated from loved ones so long, so far away and now there was Mac to introduce to the relatives. Daddy applied for transfer to Jacksonville

Naval Air Station and the wait began. Lamar and Lola found an apartment in Norfolk, leaving room for Woodrow Wilson Carter, his wife, Blanche, and daughters, Juanelle and Harriett, to move in with us. They sold their Gingham Inn in Georgia and came north looking for work.

The Carters soon moved to a rented house in New Port News, and Mother's sisters, Wilma and Mary Agnes, and cousin Delima, arrived. They found jobs but didn't stay long due to intractable home sickness. At the family gathering for Aunt Wilma's funeral in 2015, Mary Agnes answered a question about the chenille machine we had in Dixie Union; I didn't remember if we were using it in Virginia.

Aunt Mary said, "Oh, yes. My least favorite thing was to sit near the highway with the chenille spreads on a line and bring potential buyers to the house to make their purchase from Wannie." The entrepreneurial spirit accompanied us to Virginia!

A constant turnover of friends and relatives was not new or strange. All my life our home opened to all—adults in beds, children on quilt pallets on the floor—only more frequent in Virginia where there were more jobs than there were houses for new arrivals. We aided many in the human exodus from rural and small towns to centers of war-related jobs.

The influx of workers and military families caused serious overcrowding of schools. Gloria and I were transferred from Princess Anne School to Little Creek, a school near the large military base named Amphibious Training Base at Little Creek. The boggy bean field near the bay where Uncle Lamar worked was ideal. Four bases were constructed but conditions were brutal until structures were built for the troops and training methods developed. This is the meadow near where Uncle Lamar dredged canals between field and bay, where our school bus followed a two-lane road that cut through the fields. There were many sizable haystacks—strange to me because our farm never made them. One afternoon as the bus drove through the it, all the haystacks suddenly burst apart and soldiers ran out carrying rifles, one soldier per stack. On a later afternoon as the bus approached that area, the field was bathed by the end of a huge rainbow as we watched in amazement. We thought it was a lucky omen, but there was no pot of gold in sight.

Adults were not alone in facing the training for war. A drill sergeant came to the school weekly to teach us how to march following his commands, chanting, "Left, left, left my wife and twenty-three children. Left, left ... " We were taught in class to knit olive green wool scarves for soldiers headed to cold climates. Once, as we knitted, we heard an airplane's loud sputtering engine. We spontaneously rushed to the tall windows lining the exterior wall. Black smoke billowed past and we watched in horror as a fighter plane crashed and exploded in a pasture across the road. There was no survivor and I do not remember what announcement, if any, was made. We finished the school day and went home on the bus as usual. A stoicism pervaded the times and, though I never heard it expressed, it seemed our patriotic duty to not complain.

I experienced mild discrimination (I didn't know the word then) at Little Creek School when, during recess, I lined up to join the rope jumping activity. When it was my turn to jump, a classmate made an announcement.

"You can't jump on my rope," she said. "I'm from North Carolina and you're from Georgia."

Emphasis was on Georgia, shouted disparagingly.

"What's wrong with Georgia?" I wondered. "I love it."

Not wanting to cause trouble, I left the line and joined two Mennonite girls sitting on a nearby curb. I didn't know if they were banned by 'Miss North Carolina,' or whether their long black dresses made jumping rope impossible. I asked if they got haircuts, a lot of coiled hair was visible through the thin white fabric of their caps. They suggested we go to the bathroom and they would show me their hair. I was amazed to see their braids reached almost to their knees.

These girls—quiet, pleasant, and pretty—said they were not hot in their long sleeve dresses, stockings, and heavy shoes, but I knew I could not stand to be dressed that way in warm weather. The Mennonite boys were a strange sight in their high-water pants, boxy jackets, flat-top wide brim hats, and brogan shoes. Their garb struck me as unattractive and impractical.

These quiet children were transported to and from school by horse and buggy. I never heard anyone tease or bully the Mennonites and I don't remember seeing even one black child or adult during the year we were in Virginia.

Our fourth-grade teacher, often late due to morning sickness, prompted the office secretary to ask me to read to the class until she arrived. I don't remember the name of the book but several pages were read by the teacher first thing each morning and I felt honored to be the reader in her absences. It restored any lost self-esteem following Miss N.C. and her jump rope. I was not yet five years old when I learned to read in Dixie Union; I considered myself the teacher's helper. Reading to the class was perfectly normal.

To our delight, Daddy's transfer to Jacksonville NAS came through in October, soon after my tenth birthday, to report November 1. The packing and winnowing began; family and possessions must once again fit in our car for the return south. Our rented houses were furnished, but bedding, clothing, kitchen equipment, tools, and myriad items for a large family made a giant stack. Books, toys, and other non-essentials were given away.

We kept our only expensive purchase: a console radio, record player, recorder with microphone. The first record purchased had *Don't Fence Me In* on one side and *Home on the Range* on the reverse. We believed we tricked guests by taking the microphone with its long cord to another room and, through the radio's speakers, call a person's name in connection with some made-up felony. We had hours of entertainment; grownups patiently seated near the radio and children in another room, singing and 'playing' the comb. When Woodrow Carter came to visit, Daddy joined the fun with a radio announcement by the 'police' on the lookout for a dangerous suspect from Dixie Union, Ga., believed to be in the area. It worked once, briefly, as a joke. It was a time of families and friends enjoying simple pleasures, unaware the potential for danger lay close at hand.

Moving day arrived. Heavy, hard, and lumpy items went first onto the floor of the car's backseat with clothing packed in, between, around, and on top. Towels, kitchen and bed linens, blankets, quilts, and pillows filled the back seat, leaving about two feet of head room for the four children who would ride hundreds of miles prone on the bedding. Daddy, Mother and Mac occupied the front seat with snacks, lunch, and miscellaneous items that would not squeeze in the back. Goodbyes said, gas rationing coupons in hand, we set off in our overloaded car with worn tires (new ones almost non-existent for civilian use), destination: the Taylor farm in Alma.

Driving west from Norfolk we reached the familiar U.S. Highway 1, turned left and headed south, giddy, thinking of loved ones waiting.

After fifty or sixty miles, the novelty of looking out the windows wore off and singing took over. Everyone joined and we went through our repertoire of *Down in the Valley*, *Froggy Went A-Courtin'*, *You Are My Sunshine*, others, before singing became tiresome. The long ride south, lying on our possessions, was tolerated without too many complaints; longing to see our grandparents after nearly a year apart out-weighed temporary discomfort.

When Daddy stopped for gas, we tumbled out to visit the restroom and stretch our legs. Mother produced a cookie or sandwich from the lunch basket, then we squeezed ourselves back into our prone positions.

Switching drivers, Mother drove as the sun faded while Daddy slept for a few hours and the backseat passengers settled into sleep. We rolled uneventfully through the night. The sun rose over Welcome to South Carolina and the sleepy heads began a litany of "I'm hungry," and "I really, really have to go to the bathroom." The search was on for a café and a place to purchase gasoline. The car stopped at *Mama's Café and Tourist Court*, advertising "Home Cooking and Clean Cabins." We scrambled out, dashing to the restroom. *Mama's Cafe* limited fuel purchases to ten gallons, not enough to reach Alma. Service stations along the route displaying handmade "Out of Gas" signs increased as we traveled south.

Knowing we would reach Georgia and our Taylor grandparents before the day was over, we barely contained our excitement. With many miles ahead Daddy worried about the miles per gallon. All eyes watched for gas signs as the fuel indicator dropped lower. Then it happened. The car sputtered and rolled to a stop a few miles over the Georgia line on a desolate stretch with no stores or houses in sight and few vehicles on the road. We were happy to have relief from cramped quarters and to see a carpet of shiny brown needles under the familiar tall and majestic long leaf pines. We played chase and Mother walked around holding Mac. Daddy lifted the car's hood to indicate a problem, not simply a rest stop.

After many minutes, the need for food and a bathroom increased. Running around beneath the pines lost its excitement; hunger set in. Suddenly, Daddy held up his hand, a signal to be quiet as he walked to the edge of the pavement.

"I hear a big truck and I'm going to wave it down. You children stay back to give the driver room to pull off."

Daddy stepped onto the pavement, waving his hands and, as the truck slowed, we could hardly believe our eyes. It was a gasoline tank truck.

"I have to account for every gallon," the driver said. "It's going to a location about ten miles ahead."

A brief silence, Daddy scratching his head, looking down, chopping at the hard-packed dirt with the toe of his shoe, the driver could not ignore the hopeful faces of four children, a mother holding a four-month-old infant, and a determined father pleading his case. Daddy continued to stand at the truck's front bumper with no intention of moving. The driver couldn't resist; said he might be in trouble with his boss but he let us buy enough gas to get to Alma. Daddy gave the driver money and gas stamps, thanked him and we were on our way.

The prospect of spending the night on the road had clearly worried our parents if we should be stranded. Cell phone development was decades away, almost no cars on the road, no discernible structures in view and the sun dipping behind the pines, the picture was grim. The arrival of the gas truck was a miracle.

Finally, "Alma, 15 miles" appeared, tilted at an angle among the feathery green dog fennels. The old farmhouse finally came into view. Daddy tapped the horn repeatedly, making the familiar left turn onto the dirt lane. Our grandparents, arms outstretched in welcome, hurried down the porch steps. Flanked by tall cedars, clean white sand covering the bare dirt, the front gate with the weighted chain automatically closing against farm animals that might eat the flowers; we were home. A visit to the outhouse, washing up at the back porch wash stand, eating a favorite dessert—spice cake with cream filling—and a glass of Jersey-rich raw milk, put us in our familiar world with war far away. I wanted to explore, to check out the tobacco barn, corn crib, smoke house, scuppernong grape arbor, Jackson's crossing at the branch where, according to folklore, Andrew Jackson crossed on his way to Florida. Everything was just as we left it in December, 1941.

Jacksonville housing shortage required us to stay at the farm while Daddy once again searched for a house. He lived in a boarding house—spent weekends with us—leaving for work early on Mondays. We enrolled in the Alma schools we left a year ago, before our experience and knowledge leapt beyond the confines of Alma and Dixie Union. Gloria and I are second and fourth graders, James and Jerry too young for school.

Bobby stayed in Waycross where he attended school and made visits to the farm. Recalling these frequent periods of separation helped me understand why he never seemed totally part of our family. He liked Waycross where numerous cousins, even aunts and uncles his age were companions. Grandmother Mary Jane was having babies while her older daughters—Mother among them—were having babies. At the Sweat residence, we were one of many children, not as special as we were at the Taylors where we, and Jeannett's son, Larry, were the only grandchildren. Mother was the lone member of her family to move away; her ten living siblings remained in Waycross. Many founded small businesses; there were no farmers in that generation of relatives. Mother was barely in her teens when her brothers, Horace and Joseph, were killed in a car/train wreck three blocks from their home. Aunt Annie, driving the car, survived but spent many weeks in the hospital. Throughout our lives, Mother warned us to look out for trains at every railroad crossing.

In 1942, water for the farm was drawn up in a bucket, cold, with a taste of moss. There was no phone; electricity had expanded to include a few wall outlets allowing music to come into the house. The unpopular outhouse, twenty yards from the back porch past the old black walnut tree was still used.

We did not know how long the farm would again be our home before moving to another strange city eighty miles south on U.S. Highway 1. The packed car, now emptied of its cargo, left for Jacksonville at daylight. Once more, Daddy lived in a boarding house, spent evenings searching for a house to buy with money saved in Virginia, and visited the farm on weekends. Finding a house in another overcrowded Navy town was challenging. Families arrived daily hoping to find a place to live with a loved one who might be sent overseas at any moment.

In a few months' time, Daddy found a house he could afford to purchase in an area on Jacksonville's westside called Kempsville. It contained one bathroom and two bedrooms; the living room became the boy's bedroom with a bed but no couch. We knew the drill and soon the necessities were loaded. I was glad to learn we would be only a couple of hours away from our grandparents and other relatives. Like the band of highway gypsies, we were on the road again.

We drove south on the historic U.S. Highway 1 that bordered the farm of my grandparents, that always lead us 'home' when schedules permitted or circumstances required.

Chapter Three

Growing up in Jacksonville

"Joyce was a well-behaved student before you got here," said Miss Wright, fifth grade teacher.

I was humiliated. She was the only teacher I ever disliked. Joyce Kirkland, seated next to me asked where I was from. I only whispered "Norfolk" but she kept asking questions I tried to ignore. Thus began my miserable months in class 5A at Thomas Jefferson School. In the Florida system students spent the first half year in class B, followed by class A in a different room with a different teacher. If someone failed, it was for half, not a whole year. Additionally, students who excelled could skip B and begin the year in Class A. I enrolled in 5A near the end of the school year.

Summer vacation arrived. Miss Wright presented my report card with the comment, "You don't deserve to pass, but I'm going to let you try sixth grade." I worried all summer about sixth grade. I had no idea why Miss Wright disliked me, never said a kind word while I did everything she asked. I didn't tell my parents about this; I didn't want them to worry, to think I was in trouble. Many adults—like that teacher—have no idea the harm words can cause a child. Eighty-plus years later, I still remember my cheeks red with embarrassment, chastised in front of the class, my first day in a new school environment.

Fall came and two weeks into class 6B, my teacher said, "You should skip this first half and advance to 6A. You need more challenge than this class provides." I was on cloud nine in 6A with a wonderful teacher, Mrs. Shoemake. My summer of dread was over and I was relieved to know I was not a bad, stupid student. On her blackboard were two quotes: "It matters not if you win or lose, but how you play the game," and "Fill every minute with sixty seconds of distance run." Those thoughts, imprinted on my brain, kept me focused through the decades.

Unfortunately for my children, they grew up hearing too much, "Hurry, let's finish this job. We have something else to do."

During the summer I grew rapidly and except for one boy, I was the tallest kid in 6A. I thought I was doomed to be a giant and never have a boyfriend! Before year's end, I had two "older boyfriends" from the seventh grade: Eugene McLeod brought me Hershey chocolate bars with almonds, and Reddick Lyons gave me his silver identification bracelet which I hid in my room. I knew Daddy would not let me keep it. One evening Reddick caught me off guard with a quick kiss on my lips when he walked me two blocks home from Baptist Training Union. I was speechless over his brazenness and decided to keep my guard up. There was no more kissing for a few years.

The church nearest our house was Baptist, attended by some of my classmates, and I went there for socializing with friends. I did not take church or religion seriously. The preacher said playing cards, dancing, and drinking were sins; I knew my parents were upstanding people who did all three of these "sinful" activities. It was thirty years before I joined the Episcopal Church where these pleasures were not labeled sinful.

There had been no discussion about my maturing eleven-year-old body by family, teacher, or doctor—I had never been to a doctor—and the mild stomach cramps I experienced didn't seem important. I was embarrassed when a female classmate said to me, "You need a bra."

I told Mother this and about the cramps and she said, "You're just growing up." I suppose she was trying to start a conversation about puberty but I left the room angry, thinking she dismissed my feelings. The subject never came up again and an important conversation never took place. She took me to the store for the bra and, unknown to me, she also bought sanitary pads and a belt to hold those worrisome things in place. My first period came soon and it was a shock to me. I was incredibly ignorant.

A cousin asked, "Are you glad you have your period?"

My answer was "I guess so. Might as well get it over." I thought it was a one-time occurrence.

The cousin informed me, "It's going to happen every month until you are an old lady and now you can have babies."

"This is so unfair!" I said.

I was not happy. I had made no connection between bleeding and babies. A modern eleven-year-old would laugh at such misinformation.

In Jacksonville, the war was far away; children insulated against harsh reality. There were no ships in a nighttime convoy nor did sergeants teach us to march. My parents worried about a letter from the draft board; Daddy's status was upgraded to 1-A in spite of color blindness, a hernia, six dependent children, and his critical work for the Navy. He drove to Waycross, where he registered in 1942. I don't know what he was told about his chances of being "called up" but he bought a bottle of whiskey and drank it as he returned home. A few blocks from our house, he passed out and drove into the ditch. The school bus route passed the scene and all the children were excited to see a car in the ditch. I was humiliated and made no sound; I was not sure if my friends recognized that the driver was my father. At our bus stop, I ran in the house shouting, "I hate Daddy. I hate Daddy." Bobby slapped me hard on the cheek and said, "Don't ever say anything like that again." I went to my room crying, wondering what my friends knew about the man in the ditch. No one at school mentioned the incident; Mother did not complain, Daddy was never drafted, and I got over the embarrassment.

The car in the ditch was the second indication Daddy sometimes drank too much though he kept it hidden. Our house had one bathroom and it contained a closet where dirty clothes were thrown on the floor before a bath. One morning I went to the bathroom and found Daddy asleep with his 6' 2" frame squeezed into the closet atop the pile of dirty clothes. In the kitchen, Mother calmly made breakfast. I asked her what was wrong with Daddy and she told me with no trace of anger or judgement.

"Last night your Daddy came home smelling like a whiskey barrel," she said. "I told him no one smelling like that could sleep in bed with me."

Daddy soon untangled himself from the dirty clothes, showed up in the kitchen and ate breakfast. No one said a cross word, and all was well with the world. I can't remember either parent ever raising a voice in anger at the other although there were many differences of opinion. This seemed impossible, but when I asked my younger siblings if they ever heard one of our parents speak loudly or harshly to the other, their answers also were "no."

I would be furious if my husband came home with whiskey on his breath. There is a country song about this: "Don't come home a-drinkin' with lovin' on your mind." I smile when I hear it because in memory I see tall Daddy, soundly asleep on the dirty clothes, legs bent like a pyramid, in a cramped closet with no door to hide his shame. He and his old buddy, Woodrow Carter, had stopped for a beer—and a few more—after work.

Daddy tested airplane engines and once again we were on a waiting list for a home telephone and automobile tires. We were lucky he found a house to buy, cutting short our stay at the Alma farm. The Carters left Norfolk after we came to Florida and once again stayed with us while Woodrow obtained work. Gloria and I were happy to have our friends, Juanelle and Harriet, back with us.

Instead of waiting for a house to rent, Woodrow, with Daddy's help (after his workday at NAS), built an addition of two bedrooms, a kitchen, and bath onto the back of our five room one bath home. An enclosed porch connected the two living areas. Wartime necessitated creativity, and odd housing arrangements often helped solve housing shortages.

An area nearby became the neighborhood playground with a creek and swimming hole where Taylor and Carter children spent carefree summer hours. Bobby's friend, fifteen or sixteen years old, was with us when he said for all to hear, "Bobby, don't you think Norma Jeanne has pretty legs?"

Bobby's reluctant reply: "I guess so."

I was embarrassed, blushed, but inwardly I was thrilled to be noticed by an 'older' boy.

In 1945, Lynda was born while we were at school. Once again, no mention of an impending birth, just a big surprise when we arrived home. Each day, Daddy would pick up a woman from the "quarters" to help Mother take care of baby Lynda and cook. I asked her if she wanted to be referred to as a negro, or with some other word. This was a month before my twelfth birthday and I clearly remember her response.

"We want to be referred to as colored persons," she said. "We are persons."

That was eighty plus years ago, long before "Black is beautiful" became a mantra. I didn't realize it then but that quiet statement informed my understanding of appropriate designation. I once referred to her as a "colored lady," and I was pulled aside and corrected.

"It is correct to say white lady and colored woman," said one of Mother's sisters.

Juanelle Carter, more "worldly" about sex, confided she knew how babies were made, that "daddies put their 'thing' into a woman between her legs and later a baby comes out."

This brief description was reminiscent of the rabbits in Norfolk. We wondered how that would feel and decided to find something to substitute for a man's "thing." We hit upon the idea of the attachments to a douchebag/hot water bottle in the bathroom closet. When no one was around, we carried the attachments into a bedroom and took turns attempting to insert the larger one into our bodies. The tube didn't go in far, didn't feel pleasurable, and we quickly decided adults were crazy if they liked doing something that felt like that.

It's obvious I received no sex education from reliable sources and I was prudish with boys; not even dry-lip kissing after that one surprise kiss from Reddick. I sensed it could lead to unwanted behavior from anxious boys and I was not interested in testing that theory. Besides, Mother and Daddy kept us on a short rope, knew who we were with, where, and what we were doing, always in a group, leaving scant opportunity for any misbehavior.

I entered eighth grade at Robert E. Lee High School; there was no separate middle school. It shocked me to see high school girls smoking in the bathrooms. Clustered in threes or fours, they puffed madly, giggling, in the white-tiled room with its high windows above a row of stalls, basins along the opposite wall, as awestruck eighth graders gaped. Some of my classmates believed it was sophisticated, looked glamorous like movie stars, and they planned to sneak cigarettes from older brothers or fathers. I decided I would never smoke; it smelled bad, the smoke made my eyes water, and I thought smoking looked cheap. I was smug as my friends tried to smoke with teary eyes, burning throat, and coughing. They believed they were worldly grownups and I thought they looked ridiculous. I was what my children derisively called a goody two-shoes. I didn't want to upset my parents and I knew my conduct was a way to stay out of trouble. I wondered if my friends might not like me if I didn't join their "fun." I learned I could say no to smoking and keep my friends.

Beginning with sixth grade when I skipped 6B, I changed grades at mid-year and it felt awkward. I asked to take an upper class subject each semester instead of mandatory study hall. I wanted to gain enough credits to skip another half year, allowing me to advance in September instead of January. The decision paid off in 1948 when we moved to the farm. Georgia did not have a half-semester program and I had extra credits allowing me to skip half of ninth grade and enter the tenth. School years were happy times at Dixie Union, Alma, Norfolk, and Jacksonville, except for Miss Wright's 1942 fifth grade class.

WWII ended with great revelry throughout the nation and many families returned to places they called home. We remained in Jacksonville where Daddy wanted a business of his own. He and Woodrow built a service station/repair garage, named Woodcliff, (Woodrow and Clifford) on land purchased in the Springfield section of Jacksonville's Main Street. Initially, Woodrow ran the station, Daddy joined him when his NAS shift ended at 4 o'clock, and he worked at Woodcliff until closing. This division of labor continued a few months until the business could support two families. Daddy gave up his NAS job and devoted full time to managing Woodcliff with Woodrow in charge of automotive repair.

To call Daddy at Woodcliff, it was necessary to use the phone of an older couple next door. At dusk one evening Mother said, "I see the Arnetts have returned from grocery shopping. Run over there and ask if you may use their phone to call your Daddy."

As I approached and asked about the phone, Mrs. Arnett said, "Oh, certainly. Let me get this door unlocked."

As we entered the small, dark, windowless vestibule, she flipped the light switch; the light came on and instantly went off. "It's a blown fuse. I know where a new one is. Willard, stay here with Norma Jeanne 'til I get the lights on."

As soon as she disappeared into the dark hallway, Mr. Arnett put his arm around my shoulder, cupped his hand over my minuscule breast and gave it a squeeze. I slapped his hand away, dashed out the door, and ran home. I told Mother the lights were out and I could not use the phone in the dark. I didn't reveal what transpired but I never entered the Arnett's house again.

Years later I learned Gloria, ten years old, had a more dangerous close call. With Mrs. Arnett away, her husband lured Gloria to an upstairs bedroom under the pretense of giving her something pretty; instead, he pushed her down on a bed, but she was able to scramble out of his clutch, run downstairs and get out of the house. Gloria kept it secret, just as I did, and the old pervert got away with criminal behavior because we did not tell. Gloria felt "It must have been my fault for being there and causing the problem." I felt the same. We finally got a phone.

Long before daylight, 1947, school out for the summer, Daddy woke me with a tap on my shoulder saying Mother needed to go to Grandmother's house in Waycross. He would return as soon as he could make the 160-mile round trip. He helped Mother out the door; I could hear her softly crying. I do not remember Mother saying anything and I had no idea what was happening.

I knew she was pregnant although it had never been mentioned. I wondered if that was the problem, or perhaps Grandmother Sweat was sick. Eventually, I went back to sleep, awakened by Daddy's return and hearing "Your mother will be in Waycross with Grandmother Sweat for a couple of weeks; you will have to take care of the children. I'll be home every afternoon to help as soon as I get off work." With no more information than that, he left for work and I sat in bed wondering how I could manage to fill Mother's shoes for two whole weeks.

Even today, it is hard for me to contemplate being in charge of Lynda, twenty months old; Mac, four; Jerry, eight; James, nine; and Gloria, eleven. I was fourteen with more responsibility than I could imagine. There was no hired help and Daddy worked an eight-hour shift at NAS. We were a sight at the grocery store with all of us in tow. Whenever we left the house, everyone had to go. Daddy was the only driver; I was the only food shopper and the children couldn't be left alone.

"Pick out what you know how to cook, and get something to make my lunches," was Daddy's advice. He believed the kitchen was the province of women and I knew more about cooking than he did.

Our menu was limited but nutritious. The most common meal was boiled and buttered Irish potatoes, green beans, pork chops, and blackberry cobbler. Besides providing our dessert, the blackberries—rampant in lots nearby—provided entertainment. With a quilt and toys for baby Lynda, and buckets for the berries, we frequently set out for the berry patch. It gave everyone something to do under my watchful eye. Mac played with baby Lynda and kept her on the quilt; the rest of the little army busily picked berries. They knew it was the only way to get dessert. Daddy's lunch was often a bologna and onion slices sandwich. He never complained.

Time stood still. Preparing supper, bathing, and dressing the children for bed occupied my evenings. In the kitchen, a picture of a scantily-clad pretty woman adorned the automotive parts calendar where I marked off the days until Mother's eagerly awaited return. "I can surely manage for two weeks," was my thought. At the first week's end, Daddy drove to Waycross to see her: still no word to us as to why she was there, only upon return "she felt better."

Baby Sondra Elaine, "Sandy," arrived at the end of week two and I learned Mother must stay in bed for two more weeks before returning; a whole month of trying to do her job! We missed her terribly.

Years later, I discovered she began labor pains the night Daddy took her to her mother's home. I never asked why she cried, whether it was due to pain or because she had to entrust her precious children to a novice. Her labor stopped and resumed two weeks later. New mothers were required to have two weeks bed rest after the birth, turning the expected two-week stay into four weeks.

We were ecstatic when Daddy announced he would bring Mother and our baby sister home. Mother was thrilled to get back to her children and we were jubilant to see her; none more relieved than I. She told me she could not believe how plump everyone was; she thought I was too young and inexperienced to keep everyone properly fed. She laughed when I explained our diet of buttered potatoes and cobbler.

A second potentially dangerous man crossed my path that summer. Mother and Daddy were grocery shopping, the children were getting into bed and I was on the front porch swinging tiny baby Sondra to sleep when a man I occasionally saw in our neighborhood walked past on the sidewalk. He turned around, walked up the steps and came onto our porch. I was terrified. He started small talk and promptly squeezed in beside me on the swing, making me wary and not sure what I should do. I feared he might force me to leave the house.

"I just want to talk to you," he said.

"We can't talk right now because the baby is falling asleep," I said.

"Let me help you take her inside and put her in bed."

"No, it will just take a minute. Wait here. I'll do it."

I wanted to give the impression I would return to the porch. I walked slowly, carefully, holding Sandy then frantically locked the front door behind us. I ran to the back door, closed and locked it, my heart beating wildly as I put Sandy in her bed. After a few minutes, the man called to me to come out, "so we can talk," but I made no sound and finally he left after trying the door and finding it locked. It was another instance of thinking perhaps I should not have been on the porch, (my fault) and I never told my parents. I didn't realize my body was maturing but my brain was still "little girl acqui-escing to an adult, powerless as an individual."

Decades after its publication, I read Betty Friedan's *The Feminine Mystique*. Only then did I understand more fully the post-WWII brainwashing that led girls my age to desire marriage and children, overshadowing any thoughts of career or independence. Women felt guilty if they did not give up jobs to GI's. Many were loath to return to the role of housewife or "spinster" after experiencing the satisfaction of having money, making decisions, controlling their lives while the men were away. There was great happiness when the men returned, but there was also a sense of something lost. Many women relin-quished jobs they loved, returning with scant complaint to cooking and cleaning, avoiding the appearance of unpatriotic selfishness.

A few years later, like those patriotic women, Daddy was faced with the unwanted decision of leaving the work he loved at Woodcliff in order to keep the centuries-old land of his grandfather intact for future generations. Heartbreaking as a sale to outsiders would be for Granddaddy, it presented a dilemma for Daddy. He faced the decision of becoming a farmer—the life he left behind in 1930 and never expected or wanted to return to—or feeling he failed his father and future generations. He struggled with the decision of giving up his share of Woodcliff service station as it was prospering, where he did the work he loved, for a farm livelihood he clearly did not love. The Scots-Irish clan belief family and property must be kept intact left him with the feeling he had no choice. He wrestled with the problem but in the end, he could not let the farm be sold to a stranger. He decided he must sell his share of Woodcliff to Woodrow, buy the farm from Granddaddy, and move our family to Alma. I didn't realize the emotional tur-moil he must have felt as he weighed life changing decisions.

This was the first time I was not excited about a move. I had many friends in Jacksonville. Joyce Kirkland, the girl who got me in trouble on my first day at Thomas Jefferson School, was a close friend. Our Jacksonville house had a bathroom, and a telephone; I was aware an outhouse, well water, and no telephone waited for us at the farm.

After Daddy's decision, the family piled into our car one December Sunday to drive the familiar route north on U.S. Highway 1, tell the tenant farmer the farm was now ours and in two months we would move there. The old farmhouse looked bleak and dreary, so unlike the joyful place of my early childhood. I asked the little girl who lived there if I might use the "bathroom" although I knew there was only an outhouse. I thought "outhouse" sounded insulting. Daddy overheard my question and had a different reaction. He said nothing until we left the tenant family then scolded me for embarrassing the child by asking about a bathroom when I knew they did not have one. I remember the concern of my father who, in the midst of a conversation with a ragged tenant farmer, cared about the feelings of the farmer's child. My choice of words today is often informed by that long ago exchange.

A familiar routine began as we sold our Jacksonville house, sorted and packed household goods, called on relatives with pickup trucks to haul furniture—moving vans were for the wealthy or those without willing friends—and we headed eighty miles north to tend deep roots planted by Granddaddy in 1906 in the soil of the farm. I never heard Daddy express a word of regret over his decision but it was a difficult choice. Granddaddy was tearfully overjoyed with Daddy's purchase and spent much time with us during the ensuing years on the land where he was happiest. It was the home place where he felt grounded and always returned to after visits with relatives around Florida and Georgia. Having him with us was a pleasing walk down memory lane for me and his wisdom about farming was critical.

From my earliest memories I loved my Taylor grandparents for acts of kindness in the face of the brutal Great Depression.

Grandmother Macy selected flour sacks with a pattern suitable for a little girl and when she had three matching sacks she made me a dress. She disliked the long, droll dresses on most girls and made mine short with a matching ruffle added to my panties "in case my dress flew up while playing." I embraced her love of flowers and gardening, often my solace in troubled times. She worked the fields swathed in long sleeves, long pants, and wide-brimmed hat to keep her skin white and soft. She was a class act bereft of money, didn't complain, and sacrificed for the twins, Jack and Jeannette, who always looked their best. Uncle Jack wore his only white dress shirt to school every day by washing and starching it each night, drying it by the fireplace in winter, and rising early to iron it with irons heated at the fireplace or stove while Grandmother cooked breakfast. Jeannette was beautiful in dresses Grandmother copied from pictures in magazines.

Granddaddy Jimboy walked a mile to the store where a nickel bought a little bundle of peppermint sticks for me. He continued such kindness all his life and my love for him was boundless. In 1949 I helped raise money at Alma high school for our graduation trip to Washington. I needed $25 for food and miscellaneous expenses and Jack offered to give me $25 as my graduation present. Departure day arrived but Jack and the money had not and Daddy said he couldn't give me any money because he had a tractor payment due. High school friends drove to the farm to see if I needed a ride to town; our bus had arrived and would depart in an hour. Too embarrassed to admit I didn't have $25, I said I had stomach pains and felt I should not leave home. My disappointed friends returned to town; I was heartbroken. Granddaddy learned what happened, gave me all the cash he had, asked if I could eat on $17 and skip souvenirs. I grabbed my suitcase; Mother got the car keys and drove me to town just before the bus closed its door. My friends cheered as I entered and I was off to a great adventure, my first visit to the nation's capital. Tears fill my eyes as I write this, remembering my sweet Granddaddy.

When I got my first job ($23 pay for a 40-hour week), I saved up $25 and gave it to him, and did it two more times during the ensuing years. I never truly believed Daddy didn't have $17 to spare; perhaps he couldn't bear the thought of his sixteen-year-old first-born leaving on a trip far from his watchful eyes.

The trip to Washington increased my political interests when U.S. Representative Don Wheeler's Alma Page, Larry Bennett, introduced me to a handsome Page who accompanied me on our class cruise down the Potomac and to an amusement park the following night. The mutual attraction could go nowhere: different hometowns many miles apart, no telephone in my house, and a father who would not participate in furthering this budding interest. It was fun to contemplate and I told my school friends I wanted to marry a congressman. I had no thought of BEING a congressperson! My role models were mothers and homemakers who appeared content with their lives and that was my long-term plan when I left for Berry College, August, 1949.

Chapter Four

Deep Roots in Sandy Soil

T wo months! It felt like a long time to prepare for a move when we visited the tenant family at the farm and now, mid-January, moving day loomed large; anxiety crept in. In Alma, cousins were nearby and there were friends at the family church, Elizabeth Taylor Chapel, named for my great great grandmother. Her son, James Manning Taylor, gave the land and paid $200 to have the little white church built in 1886. There were two front doors side by side and an inside railing down the center aisle. I am told it is not accurate that men and women sat on opposite sides but it is what I remember from eighty-plus years ago. Up front, to the right of the pulpit, was an Amen Corner where a few pious men sat and spoke encouragement to the preacher who shouted, held the Bible high in the air, and mopped sweat from his glistening face. Brackets between the windows held kerosene lamps providing tepid light for evening services, attracting moths through open windows. No cushions eased hours of sitting on hard pews made from wide boards of the old growth long leaf pines shading the chapel on three sides; the west side reserved for burial plots surrounded by an iron fence.

Elizabeth Chapel, like most churches of the time, was built beside a stream. Water was critical for the mules, horses, humans and for baptisms. The itinerant preacher came once a month, preached morning and again in the evening, invited to someone's home for noon dinner, supper, and to spend the night. Some attendees camped out rather than travel by mule and wagon many miles after dark. Most stayed overnight with relatives or friends in the community.

During my childhood in Dixie Union, I stayed at the farm as often as possible. I was the first biological grandchild and I loved being with my Taylor grandparents. I remember riding to Elizabeth Chapel in a four-wheeled farm wagon, pulled by mules, Doc and Dan, chairs from the kitchen placed in the bed of the wagon. One Sunday, when I was four, returning home on the dirt road, a wagon wheel broke. The mules were unhitched and Jack, fourteen, rode bareback with me sitting behind him holding around his waist. Leading the other mule, Granddaddy, Grandmother, and Jeannette walked behind us. I was not sorry the wheel broke because I had never ridden a mule and I adored my Uncle Jack. The air was cool; a slight breeze worried the slender green needles of the long leaf pines bordering the road—a whispering sound—as we plodded home. Recalling these carefree times reminded me I loved the old farm and perhaps moving there might not be all bad.

Except for doors revealing slight traces of orange paint, the farmhouse was never painted before we moved there. The porch spanned the front, inviting anyone to relax in the rocking chairs and swing. A ten-foot-wide open center hall had one room on the right with an unfinished fireplace; we boarded up the opening. Next was a latticed wash stand and beyond was a five-foot bridge connecting the back porch to the well with its rope, pulley, and bucket. Weekly, an iceman would place a twenty-five-pound block of ice in the icebox located on the porch. In the South Georgia heat of summer, the ice always melted a day or two before the next delivery. Grandmother Macy lowered the bucket containing quart jars of milk and butter to the cool bottom of the well. The milk was never cold enough but the cool water kept it drinkable until the iceman arrived. The open hallway stopped at the pantry where Grandmother's canned fruits and vegetables were stored; sustenance for the winter. From the front porch, the left side of the open hall contained the living room with a bed, fireplace, windows on each side, and an outside scaffold. One opened the window to fetch a log for the fire from the scaffold. Jack's job was to make sure adequate logs were on the scaffold to keep the room warm until bedtime. In very cold weather, bricks were warmed on the hearth to put in the bed; wrapped in a warmed quilt I would be tucked in with a brick at my feet. Two bedrooms opened off the hall; last was the kitchen with a large dining table. The heat from the wood stove was welcome in winter and dreaded in summer. Built-in warming ovens above the stove's cooking area kept food warm. While the food cooked, a reservoir on the side heated water for dishwashing. A big oven baked biscuits, pies, and legendary cakes. Little did we suspect this old house, unchanged through the decades, would one day be our home.

The first farm management changes in nearly a hundred years were responses to WWII. Jack joined the Army. Daddy, Lamar, and Jeannette were married and had their own homes. Jeannette, 16, married Eldon Smith and moved to a house on Sugar Creek, several miles from family. While hospitalized during Larry's birth, she heard Eldon enjoyed a night out, dancing, and she returned to her parents' home with her baby, never to live with Eldon again. My grandparents, Jeannette, and Larry, moved from the farm to St. Simons Island for jobs in 1943.

Granddaddy worked at the Brunswick Shipyard and Jeannette worked in an office. Grandmother kept house and looked after little Larry. A sharecropper family took over operating the farm but they were inadequate custodians of the land and were not experienced at farming. The soil became deeply eroded.

No improvements were made then or in the following years. There was electricity but still no bathroom, only an outhouse with its pungent fragrance. Once again, we traveled the U.S. Highway 1 artery, north from Jacksonville to the farm. Years earlier we temporarily attended schools in Alma, waiting for the move to Norfolk; this time it would be for the rest of our primary and secondary school years. I understood Daddy's love and feeling of responsibility for the home place but I thought this step was backward for our family.

Granddaddy Jimboy came to help with the farming. Luck was not with us as rainfall, one month after we moved in, caused a historic Satilla River crest of 22.40 feet on March 4, 1948, flooding our fields at planting time although the farm was miles from the river. The rains kept coming, the new Ford tractor, bought on time, sat idle under the barn shed.

"If it was me," Granddaddy said. "I'd take that contraption back and get a decent pair of mules. Mules don't bog down like tractors."

"Yes, but they eat twelve months of the year whether they work or not, and the rain will surely stop," Daddy replied. "If it doesn't, we better forget farming and start building an ark."

By late March the soil dried out enough to work the land and plant the crops. Prepared first was a tobacco seed bed. Soon hundreds of tiny seedlings popped up, the bed covered with wide strips of thin white fabric called, appropriately, tobacco cloth, rolled back in warm sunshine, replaced on cool nights. Tobacco seedlings, a few inches high, were transplanted in prepared rows in big fields and our family formed an assembly line. Daddy made holes four feet apart with the pointed end of a dowel, Mother dropped in a seedling, James covered the hole with soil, and I settled the roots by watering from containers of well water. Machines now do this work in minutes instead of days.

Gloria was assigned to stay in the house or yard to look after the little children—Mac, Lynda, and Sandy. It felt like a game as we fell into a rhythm and moved quickly along. After a dozen or so holes, Mother stopped.

"Clifford, I think the holes are getting too deep."

"No," Daddy replied. "I think they're about right."

Mother inclined her ear toward the hole, and with a quizzical look on her face, she looked back at Daddy.

"Then why do I hear Chinese being spoken?"

My parents rarely argued about anything; Daddy usually just said no and that was the end of discussion except for Mother's responses with her unfailing sense of humor.

I entered Bacon County High School February 4, 1948, wondering if I would receive any Valentines, an old-fashioned indicator of one's popularity. A stack of pretty cards on my desk ended my concern. My best friends were my beautiful second cousins: Carol Taylor who was Miss Georgia, 1951, and her sister, Chris, Southeast Maid of Cotton, 1952. They were the "Scarletts" of Alma. On Sunday afternoons their front porch filled with boys vying for their attention and it was my good fortune to be included. Their mother, 'Aunt' Lois, was a genius keeping randy boys at bay: hand cranking the wooden ice cream churn, checking the peanuts boiling in the iron wash tub, cutting firewood, and numerous small chores. As the sun sank below the tall pines, she asked one of her daughters to play the piano so she could hear "all your beautiful young voices singing before we are out of time." This was her way of signaling when the music ends, it's time for boys to depart. Actual dating was months away.

Our farm chores were not onerous; we worked in teams and our parents were easy on us. Tobacco and cotton were the primary cash crops, demanding hard work in June through August with no air-conditioned space as refuge. We rested under the enormous canopy of Stewart pecan trees surrounding the house and outbuildings, planted by newlywed Granddaddy Jimboy around 1906, spaced fifty feet apart in each direction. I loved those trees, shade in summer and still producing nuts more than a hundred years later. Pecans were picked up and hauled in car trunks to Atlanta, Rome, LaGrange; places far

and near where progeny settled. I disliked the growing popularity of pronouncing the nuts "puh kons." I heard this change
came because pecan sounded like cans placed under the bed
at night to avoid a trip to a dark outhouse. Incorrect! Those
containers under the beds were "chamber pots" or, for the
crude, "slop jars." I preferred a simple "pecan," short "e" accent
on "can;" others may continue with whatever suits them ...but
"puh kon" is not the king's English and I considered it perhaps
an affectation by some who placed a silk blanket over their
burlap upbringing. As long as I received the delicious nuts, I
didn't care what they were called.

A vegetable garden fed us and provided a surplus to share or
sell to grocery stores. My least favorite chore—every other day
in season—was cutting the fast-growing okra which made my
skin itch. Cutting began before the sun was high and Daddy
would have a bushel of freshly gathered okra in a grocery store
by 8 a.m. There were other surplus vegetables to sell or share.
The array made a vegetarian's mouth water: tomatoes, cu-
cumbers, peas, beans, squash, potatoes, corn, peppers, water-
melons, cantaloupes, greens, pears and two grape arbors. No
longer were people planting Victory Gardens in back yards but
food was still generously shared with neighbors and visiting
friends. The work of maintaining gardens was easy compared
to the killing labor of raising cotton and tobacco.

One hot summer day tranquility was shattered. Mother and
I filled the back porch washing machine, the kind with two
rollers above and a hand crank to squeeze water out as you
fed the clothing through the rollers. Two zinc tubs for rinsing
were filled with buckets of water. We were putting dirty clothes
in the washer when a jarringly loud flapping noise filled the
air. Through the pecan canopy we saw a helicopter—pour-
ing acrid black smoke—pass low over our house and make a
bumpy landing in the small pasture between the house and
U.S. Highway 1.

Two men dashed toward the house yelling, "Water, water! Do you have a water hose?"

Mother yelled, "No, but I have two tubs filled with water."

Each man rushed up our back steps, grabbed one of those heavy tubs and sloshed his way to the burning machine, successfully putting out the fire. I could scarcely believe their luck and timing; ten minutes later those tubs would have been filled with wet clothing. We were extremely lucky; the helicopter barely cleared the huge pecan trees directly in their path and landed thirty yards from our house. Ten feet lower, they would have crashed onto our house setting it—and us—on fire. An explosion might have reached the nearby tank of gas kept on hand for the tractor, sending us and the historic farm house into oblivion.

Few people had a close-up view of a helicopter in 1949; but for three days, while waiting for a mechanic and parts, cars crowded the shoulders of U.S. Highway 1. Gawkers tramped through our pasture staring at the oddity, shaking their heads in disbelief. The name of a farm with an Iowa address was painted on the door. Daddy drove the pilot and passenger to a motel in Waycross where they waited until the repair allowed them to return to Iowa. Within a few days, the helicopter lifted off and headed north. I don't recall anyone expressing appreciation for a ride to the hotel, twenty-six miles, concern for trampling the pasture, or interruption of wash day and the work of refilling those tubs with water from the well. We were glad to help because it was the right thing, the thing Southerners were known for. Perhaps someone expressed appreciation out of my presence.

Before today's mechanization, the harvesting and barn curing processes of tobacco required many "hands," especially on tobacco picking day—the weekly chore of harvesting the mature leaves. Loaded on flat sleds, the four-foot-long leaves were brought to a covered shed attached to the curing barn. A stringer, usually a teenage girl, secured a four-foot-long to-

bacco stick into a slot, and with the help of a hander on each
side, tied alternate clumps of leaves to the stick. I was not fast
enough to be a stringer; hander was my job. Three or four
such teams were the key to a smooth operation. An efficient
three-person team could tie the leaves onto the entire stick in
less than two minutes then call "stick off," whereupon one of
several boys or men would take the filled stick into the multi-
level barn and pass it up to waiting helpers straddling the poles
in the upper tiers. Starting at the highest levels, the sticks were
laid across poles, filling a tier, then the worker would move
down and repeat the process until all tiers of the tall, square
barn were filled with the green leaves ready for curing. Timing
and skill created an operation as smooth as a well-tuned orchestra. Teenaged boys delighted in collecting the large bright
green tobacco worms with a scarlet spike on their head and
putting them in the girls' hair or dropping them down the back
of a T-shirt. The worms were quite pretty and harmless but all
those feet creeping down one's back sent the victim yelling for
help.

A fire built in a ground level brick oven, accessed from outside the barn, began the curing process. For six days and nights,
the fire and tiers of leaves were carefully monitored. Near the
end of the curing process, a dry, shrunken leaf could escape the
string, fall on the hot oven, burst into flame, and destroy the
entire contents and the barn in a matter of minutes. Not only
would the barn have to be rebuilt, about one-fifth of the year's
anticipated income would be lost. This tragedy occurred once
during our farm years. Frantic horns sounded from an eigh-
teen-wheeler on U.S. Highway 1, woke the sleeping household
to the sight of flickering bright red reflected through windows
and screen doors.

A mad dash ensued to get the gas storage tank farther from
the house and barn to prevent an explosion and to toss water
on the roof of the house as the air filled with sparks and bits

of flaming debris. The barn was totally engulfed in flames; all efforts were to save the house.

A bumper crop that season caused a change in plans. Daddy arranged to rent a larger empty barn on a nearby farm, a barn he insured against loss. Even that barn did not hold all the tobacco and a last-minute decision was made to also use the uninsured barn where the loss occurred. Clad in our night clothes we could only watch, mesmerized, thinking of the months of hard work and lost income going up in flames. The barn was not rebuilt; the farm became Coolbreeze Dairy.

A milking parlor (yes, that is what it is called), was built including electric milking machines and feeding slots for a herd of Holstein cattle. The work was somewhat easier than growing cotton and tobacco but the downside was milking morning and evening seven days a week. All schedules gave precedence to milking before dawn and again in the afternoon. Cows were expensive and failing to milk on the right schedule could lead to mastitis. There would be no more trips with all the family until we could afford hired help. At least two people were necessary to do the milking. James, Jerry, and Mac managed the chores at daylight and again after school. The milk went from a cow's udder through tubes to a large cooling tank, collected by Pet Dairy trucks every other day. Mac was a jokester and loved it when one of his four sisters was sent to the cooler to get a pitcher of milk for the house. No matter how quietly we tried to slip in, Mac loved to hit us in the face with a warm stream of milk directly from the cow; his aim was always perfect.

Daddy was an outstanding farmer; he followed the county agent's advice and read agriculture department pamphlets. He took the work in stride, never bemoaning the fact he would rather be running Woodcliff service station. He made the best of a life foisted upon him by fate.

In the beginning of Coolbreeze Dairy, a veterinarian inseminated the cows until Daddy could afford to buy a well-bred bull to help upgrade the herd. In due time a huge, intimidating bull was in the pasture with the cows that were coming 'in season.' The bull approached and mounted a cow, shoved her into the nearby electric fence, knocked both to the ground and left a fear the poor bull never overcame. As each cow came in season, the bull bellowed, swung his massive head side to side, drool flying, pawed the ground, and never mounted another cow. After several months and no improvement, Daddy reluctantly sold his expensive bull at a cheap price to be slaughtered for dog meat. We got another bull; this one was luckier with the "ladies of the pasture."

James, Jerry, Gloria, and I rode the bus to school while Mac, Lynda, and Sandy—still no kindergarten—stayed home with Mother. After graduating from Robert E. Lee High in Jacksonville, Bobby joined the Army separating himself from the family before the move to the farm. Reluctantly, our parents gave in to his pleading and signed his enlistment papers; he had just turned seventeen. It was then he learned he had a different biological father whose name was listed on his birth certificate. Bobby seemed unmoved by the discovery.

Among our brood of eight children, Bobby was unique, distant, more talented than the rest of us. He out-jitterbugged everyone with moves that I would one day see Sammy Davis, Jr. perform, and he possessed a beautiful singing voice. His athleticism allowed him to excel in sports in spite of being only five feet seven inches tall; his three younger step-brothers would reach more than six feet two inches tall but their afternoon milking schedule meant sports were never an option for them. Sandy was the athletic star of the family.

Bobby deployed to South Korea during that conflict, then to Germany where he met and married Matilda "Tilly" Kaiser and adopted her young son, Tommy. Petite Tilly, barely four and a half feet tall, and Tommy, stayed at the farm while a house was located near the Army base in Albany, Ga. where Bobby was stationed. When Tommy grew to be well over six feet tall, he questioned his mother about his height with two short parents. Finally, she admitted his father was a Polish Intelligence Officer stationed in her German town during WWII. Tommy wanted to discover the identity of his birth father but that was not to be. Following a spirited basketball game with young players he died of a heart attack in his forties. He was a loving man and we miss him terribly. Bobby drank heavily and died in a military hospital in Florida on July 4, 1985. He and Tilly were divorced; both remarried. Tommy stayed at the farm to complete his education as his parents went in different directions. He married Jane Lee and they had two outstanding children, Thomas, a Navy officer pilot, and Jessica, a school teacher.

The rest of us were finding our own path. I was a cheerleader; Gloria was a basketball player, Lynda was a majorette, Sandy was an all-star basketball player. James, Mac, and Jerry's dairy chores before and after school left no time for participation in sports. Daddy kept a tight rein on all of us, especially his four daughters. Finally, he gave in to my pleading for permission to date. During the summer before my senior high school year, I could double date on Friday and Saturday nights with an eleven o'clock curfew. Mother went to sleep when I was out; in bed, Daddy waited up. I saw the red glow stubbed out on his cigarette as I rushed through the door ten or fifteen minutes late. He never went to sleep until I was "under his roof."

James entered the air force, Jerry and Jeanne Holland eloped while they were still in high school and I dated but never went "steady" until Carlos Greenway came into my life during my senior school year. Carlos earned a degree in Landscape Architecture from the University of Georgia, received a 1949 yellow Chevrolet convertible as a graduation present, and was ten years older than I. He was drafted in 1942, served four years before entering college. He graduated college the same year I graduated high school. We met at a basketball game where he introduced himself and commented on my role as captain of the cheerleaders.

He became a mentor, introducing me to the music of jazz greats Bunny Berrigan, Bix Beiderbecke and others, taught me to play bridge, asked my opinion on landscape designs he created for clients, and I fell in sixteen-year-old love. He also introduced me to sex. On a warm summer night, top down on the convertible, dinner at the Green Frog restaurant in Waycross, he leisurely drove the twenty-six miles back to Alma with the radio tuned to WAYX, the only station with occasional classical music. He turned onto a country road lined with giant pines scenting the cool air, a slight breeze rustling the needles. I could not resist this kind, gentle, interesting person who, I imagined, would soon be my perfect husband. The leather seats still had the new car smell and there, under the millions of stars visible when there is no ambient light, it happened. It was pleasant enough but there was no ecstatic revelation; I would remember the experience later when I heard Peggy Lee sing *Is That All There Is*. Thoughts of leaving in August for Berry College began to recede when Carlos showed me a plan for a building that he would erect on property adjacent to his parents. A three-car garage and office would occupy the ground floor with a spacious apartment above. He asked my opinion about colors and appliances and I hoped I would soon look like the ecstatically happy wives in the magazine ads. I said nothing to him about my girlish fantasy and he didn't propose marriage. He continued to encourage me to follow my dream of attending Berry College.

Before I saw that building plan, the supper conversation at home would circle back to "When I get to Berry ..." followed by Daddy's, "You sure are looking way ahead. I figure about eighteen to twenty is the right age to leave home."

"Daddy. If I sit around here for four years, I'll end up marrying some poor farmer and be bored to death."

I didn't mention my hope of a future with Carlos. Daddy and I didn't argue, or shout, or leave the table in tears; we each stubbornly held our position. Before the Interstate Highway system, from Alma in southeast Georgia to Rome in the northwest was a slow journey through myriad small towns, behind logging rigs and pickup trucks in no hurry to get anywhere.

Going by bus or train required numerous changes and I didn't have the fare so I searched for a free ride. My cousin Carol was going but her family would fill their car. The Tillman brothers were already at the Boys Academy but from them I learned Lewis and Calvin Hyers, whose mother was dead, were riding to Berry with their father, Clinton, and there was room for me and my one suitcase.

Berry College was my only option for two reasons: Every activity was closely monitored by staff and chaperones (acceptable for my parents) and the total cost for a work program student was five dollars submitted with the application and requisite papers. Amazingly, that five dollars and part time work five days a week for a semester covered everything for a year, including tuition, books, room and board, and uniforms worn seven days a week. I was assigned the best job on campus—conducting tours of Sunshine crafts cottage.

Assembling the required admission papers, I discovered the doctor who delivered me in 1932 didn't bother to file a birth certificate; a complicated process ensued. I obtained a social security number and letters of strong character from my school principal, minister, and two community leaders not related to me. In retrospect, I believe Daddy knew he would give in; he drove me around town with the family Bible, report cards, and statements from relatives to establish my birth date and acquire the requisite documents while he maintained I was too young to leave.

Emotionally, I was struggling with a decision to get an education, or stay in Alma hoping for a marriage proposal. To get Carlos's reaction, I "tested the water" by telling him how opposed Daddy was to my leaving home. His answer was not what I expected but was what I needed.

He said, "I'm ten years older than you and I know I've changed into a totally different person in that time. You will change in ways you can't imagine right now but that will happen. You are the kind of person I want to spend my life with, but you are not mature enough to know if I am that person for you."

I don't remember being too disappointed; the decision was made, we were still friends and I said, "Since I am leaving you should meet the new Home Economics teacher, Janice Jordan." He did, they married and were together until his death in his nineties.

On a visit to Alma a few years before he died, I phoned Carlos with an invitation to meet for coffee. Surprised and curious, he waited at a local restaurant. He must have felt relief when I said, "I want to tell you how much I appreciate the way you expanded my limited knowledge of music, landscape design, and the enjoyment of playing bridge. Not many fifteen- to sixteen-year-old farm girls had access to such information, and I thank you." I was accompanied to the restaurant by Lynda and Sandy and I didn't feel inclined to go into any other "lessons" from him. He seemed relieved, all smiles, and I was glad for the opportunity to tell him I was appreciative.

It is amazing to recall simple things so deep in the past. Preparing for Berry, Mother ordered pink flannel pajamas with matching booties from Sears & Roebuck. She didn't want me to have cold feet while I was so far north. I packed those pajamas along with the minimum necessities I needed while waiting for custom made uniforms. Three weeks after arriving, I had three pink weekday and one dress white uniform, a gym suit, a raincoat, white oxford shoes and a black wool one-piece unlined bathing suit. Female students hated the bathing suit which was similar to a man's undershirt. That embarrassing garment clung to every protrusion and crevice when wet, plus the crotch sagged away from your private area. A male student was always the lifeguard much to our chagrin. We quickly mastered the art of grabbing a towel before stepping out of the pool and making a mad dash to the dressing room.

With approaching cold weather, the white uniform and oxfords gave way to a navy-blue dress uniform and black oxfords. We looked like nurses in spring and summer and Salvation Army lassies in fall and winter. Martha Berry, the school founder, was wise in requiring uniforms at all times. She knew most of her students were financially poor and she didn't want inadequate clothing to hinder a student, or to feel shame due to clothing.

At home in Alma with the day of departure approaching, I packed my few possessions and anticipated Clinton Hyers' arrival. The supper time conversation returned to my usual, "When I get to Berry ... " and Daddy's familiar "I can't see how that's going to happen any time soon." The day before I expected to leave, Daddy said, "If you are determined to do this, I will take you. I stopped by today and told Clinton he didn't need to come to get you." I was shocked; Daddy's "No" always meant just that and I was stunned at the turn of our conversation.

We ate breakfast at dawn, said goodbye to Mother and the children. This was August and I did not realize how long it would seem and how homesick I would be before Christmas; the first-time students could leave the campus. I was most unfortunate in developing a serious bout of food poisoning at the end of my first week at Berry, hospitalized for the first time in my life, and totally alone. I was glad my family was not notified; they would have probably arrived to take me home.

Thankfully, we could not imagine I would soon be hospitalized as I began my journey. I looked back as Mother waved and wiped her tears. It pained me to cause her sadness but she wanted me to pursue my desire for an education. With the right turn onto U.S. Highway 1, we headed north to Hazelhurst where we began angling northwest through hot and dusty farmlands, crops harvested, small towns benefitting from the sale of those crops. Daddy rarely spoke and I could not think of anything appropriate to say as we rode hour after hour. "Are you thirsty?" or "Do you need a bathroom stop?" made up most of Daddy's conversation. As we approached Rome, Daddy said he was told about a place for a tasty lunch and he hoped we were not too late. He found the place; people were eating at tables on the porch, living room, and dining area. We were handed a plate, directed to the kitchen and approached the stove where our plates were filled with delicious food. It had been a long time since breakfast.

With dinner over (lunch to non-farmers), Daddy consulted his directions and we soon were at the Gates of Opportunity—the entrance to the Berry campus. No one in my family went to college and we weren't sure what we were supposed to do but the paperwork I sent was ready and we were directed to the breath-taking beauty of Ford campus. At the stone Gothic archway, Daddy retrieved my suitcase from the car's trunk and walked to the arch where he was told no males were allowed beyond the garden entrance and someone would help with my small suitcase. His sad face as he gave me a hug, one of the few ever bestowed on me—he was not a hugger—indicated how hard it was for him to leave me in a strange place among people we did not know.

He took a deep breath and slowly let it out.

"Bye," he said. "I guess I'll be leaving now."

The only tears I ever saw him shed—he had not even cried at his mother's funeral—rolled down those weathered cheeks. I was heartbroken to see sadness in a man who spent his life protecting his family from harm, stricken by my actions. For a second, I wondered if I were doing the right thing but it was too late to turn back; I waved and followed my suitcase to Mary Hall West in the Ford quadrangle.

At that moment it didn't occur to me my departure would be so permanent, never to really live at home again but it must have been in Daddy's thoughts as he could not hold back those tears. On a later visit to Alma, I ran into one of Daddy's coffee drinking buddies who said, "Your daddy is mighty proud of you. Tells everybody in Alma about you being up there in that Berry College."

I smiled at the revelation; Daddy never said it to me.

Chapter Five

Berry College, Atlanta, Jacksonville

C arlos Greenway was right. Between my Berry College arrival in August, 1949, and my first trip home at Christmas, I met popular, handsome Drexel Whiddon, a Berry senior. Holding hands or the occasional stolen kiss was the entirety of romantic encounters but I acknowledged the wisdom of Carlos's advice; I was becoming a different person.

Public school was easy; I expected a college challenge but my major was not difficult or demanding. I chose home economics to be a better wife and mother with no thought of a career. I hoped to avoid math.

Berry seemed a safe place to increase homemaker skills as I went from sixteen to eighteen, an age I foolishly believed suitable for marriage. Before Betty Friedan's game-changing book, *The Feminine Mystique* appeared, I did what the government wanted and Madison Avenue promised.

A campaign was instituted encouraging women to give up their wartime jobs. Marriage, motherhood, and accelerated consumerism were presented to teenage girls as the greatest path to happiness. Decades later, happily married to Al and pregnant with our first child, I read Friedan's book and wept. Tears were not from unhappiness but from realizing why, at sixteen, I thought more about marrying Carlos than I did about education or a career. I cried for the women who loved the jobs they gave up to become housewives; for teenage girls whose dreams of a career were abandoned.

Al woke up around 2 a.m., saw me reading and crying, and said, "If the book is that damned sad, just quit reading it."

My response was, "I have to read it to understand the poor choices I made as a teen."

Al turned over, went back to sleep; I read until dawn.

My high school and college serial dating began to make sense. I was shopping for prince charming, living happily ever after in a rose covered cottage filled with beautiful children, and buying amazing stuff. I blithely continued through a series of Berry boyfriends; no serious relationships developed. Fate frequently intervened. The Korean conflict caused many students to join ROTC and, upon graduation, they became military officers. I moved on to the next attractive beau.

Drexel Whiddon inspired the only lie I told Berry's dean of women. He invited me as his date for Senior Breakfast, a sunrise celebration at Victory Lake which—before the quarry drained it—was quite lovely. Underclass students prized a rare invitation. Matters were complicated due to my living in Mothers Memorial Building (now named Green Hall) on the boys' campus, waiting for a permanent space with the freshman girls in Mary Hall. The Dean hesitated as I asked for permission to go. She said the housemother would have to get up before dawn and chaperone me as I walked to the Ford buildings with male students and their chaperones. Finally, she said if the housemother agreed to it, I could go. She and I both believed the elderly housemother would say "No." That is what happened. On the form I presented, housemother wrote: "Norma Jeanne Taylor does not have my permission to attend Senior Breakfast." The word "not" appeared at the end of a line and I decided to get rid of the offending word. A friend in the school newsletter/photography department liked my idea and provided a chemical to erase those three little letters—NOT. A wrinkled smudge remained and as I handed the permission slip to the astonished Dean, I apologized for "spilling water on the paper."

Unknown to the sleeping elderly housemother, I walked with the chaperones and male seniors to the Ford arch where we were transported by bus to Victory Lake. A beautiful sunrise painted the lake's surface; bountiful food and ever vigilant chaperones awaited our arrival. If my obliteration of 'NOT' was discovered, it was never mentioned by the dean.

Drexel left for military service and rising senior Reginald Strickland became my partner at the Saturday night dances in the Ford gym. Reginald was also in ROTC, soon graduated and departed for a military career.

Tom Pettit, next senior student of special interest, lived on campus, the stepson of Dr. McAllister, (for whom Berry's science building is named). He was in ROTC, graduated my second year, and went directly into the Marine band as a trumpeter.

Tom's brother, Dick, was a Berry student and when we crossed paths on campus, we would exchange news from Tom. As was my usual habit, I looked directly into Dick's eyes as I listened to his report. After losing his train of thought Dick said, "I can't think when you look at me like that." I wasn't looking any special way and I realized there was power in eye contact.

"Okay, I'll look at your shoes. Is this better?" We laughed and the air was cleared.

With the discovery of the power of eye contact, I gave my roommates flirting lessons, including what to do with their eyes.

The U.S. involvement in North Korea increased and more friends in ROTC left. These relationships were not serious and I felt no sense of loss as each "beau" departed. Once I was ready to marry Carlos when I was sixteen; now it was more fun to date a lot of guys.

Oteria "Terri" Watkins, my cousin living in Atlanta, visited Berry and convinced me I should leave school, live with her and get a job where she worked. Earning my own money had a strong appeal and when I left college for Christmas break, I did not return to Berry but moved to Atlanta. Immediately, Terri took me to her work place and I was hired for a "new" position. I could begin the next day. A desk was brought in and placed in front of the glass door of Forrest E. Henderson's office. He was district manager of John Deere Plow and Implement Company's regional office and he created the new position. I was assigned to the accounting department (with limited knowledge of the subject) at a salary of $23 per week, soon raised to $28. Located in Chamblee, the modern building contained a glassed-in chilled room housing a forerunner of computers and also had 1951s newest HVAC, designed to magnetically remove pollutants from the air. I escorted visitors from the Moline home office and other dignitaries through the building explaining these technological advances. The rest of the time, I was an "accountant," recording numbers, and sometimes sitting across the desk from Forrest Henderson listening to tales of the "John Wilkes Booth Society." This organization had no rules, no dues and was apparently an excuse for several die-hard southern rebels to play cards, bad-mouth the North and reminisce about The Lost Cause. I do not remember overt racism in his tales but, in a state of naiveté, I might not have recognized such. I did however notice he was tall, handsome, charming, and married; there were photos of his family on the console behind his desk.

Terri's husband attended Atlanta Pharmacy College and worked as a druggist in the evening. It was Terri's need for companionship and fear of being alone that caused her to "recruit" me to come live with her and Elbert in their Chamblee apartment. I was an easy sell due to the lure of earning money—one thing I never had.

Georgia Tech and Emory connections were made and by February I had invitations to three formal balls to be held in May. My first purchase with my new "wealth" was made at Leon Froshin's Shop, the most expensive store in Atlanta for women's apparel. A shopper entered a lovely room with a couch, large gold framed mirror, a personal attendant to select gowns in your size and assist you in trying them on. It was an amazing experience for someone in a new job earning $23 but I wanted something stunning. I selected a coral, strapless gown with a multilayer skirt and a price tag of $95, plus $10 to hem the multilayers. It took me until May to get the gown out of layaway but I felt like Cinderella going to the ball. I wore "the dress" to the Georgia Tech dance as Jerome Bennett's date. The extravaganza, sponsored by the Georgia Tech fraternities, featured Ray Charles as headliner. The second night there was another Tech dance with jazz trumpeter, Ray Anthony, as the star. No way could I afford a second formal gown, so I made a strapless blue dress.

Two years earlier, I had made a strapless gown for my senior prom in Alma. My dress looked fine compared to the dresses of the Alma town girls. I was on the dance floor all evening. Does anyone cut-in anymore—tap your dance partner on his shoulder whereby he surrenders you to the new dance partner? I loved the occasions someone cut in to dance with me while my date stepped aside. Have today's teens enjoyed these in-nocent pleasures or has texting obliterated simple moments of joy? After the dancing ended, students converged on the Alma Debbie House for hamburgers and Cokes. I am astonished at the money spent on modern-day proms and the pressure it puts on parents and students. I wonder if today's graduates have as much fun as we did on a low budget in 1949. We never saw a limousine or ate in a restaurant with stars after the name but we had fun and no one was in debt. Did texting replace many simple, tender exchanges between teenagers?

The Georgia Tech fraternity members I met were gentlemen and treated their dates like princesses. Television was relatively new (none on the campus at Berry, few in homes) and Senator Eugene McCarthy's hearings were the hot item. We sat on sofas at the fraternity houses, the overflow on the floor, and watched the proceedings.

Phi Delta Theta was my favorite fraternity and soon I sported Jerry Bennett's pin—getting "pinned" meant engaged to become engaged. Graduation was a month away and as a member of ROTC, the day Jerry graduated he became a Navy Lieutenant and was soon on his way to Italy. Two weeks of sitting at home caused me to rethink my situation when Charlie Hager of Phi Kappa Tau fraternity invited me to a party on an estate near Stone Mountain. Jerry's frat pin came right off my dress and soon was on its way to Italy attached to a "Dear Jerry" note.

I was eighteen, obviously fickle, and loving the experience of freedom in a big city after the restrictions of Alma and two years in the Berry "bubble."

Not only were my boyfriends constantly graduating, they were leaving for faraway places and I had no intention of sitting around and waiting. Elbert completed pharmacy school and planned to return with Terri to South Georgia to his uncle's Waycross drugstore. I was about to be homeless in Atlanta.

Another single woman at John Deere suggested we share an apartment and I could stay in Atlanta. When word of that plan reached Forrest Henderson, he called me to his office. He spent an hour convincing me that was a bad idea: He told of "pitfalls waiting for young women without family around, the temptations, and gullibility leading to trouble." He asked if I had relatives in Jacksonville, nearer Alma, and I said "Yes, my Aunt Jeannette." With that, the pressure was on; he was adamant I should move there when Terri left, and abandon thoughts of staying in Atlanta.

He reminded me of Carlos's insistence I should leave Alma for college where I would become "another" person. I felt mature but in truth, I was only eighteen. As I sat across the desk and listened, I realized it was not me he didn't trust; he didn't trust himself.

In that moment, I accepted the wisdom of his advice and abandoned all thought of remaining; I didn't know if I could resist temptation. He was an attractive man, more sophisticated, more interesting than young men I knew. My work friends called me his pet. He would sometimes come into the staff dining room and sit at the table occupied by my friends and me. They insisted he never sat with employees before I arrived. I brushed it off as fatherly concern because I was the youngest employee. Listening to him plead—I think that word fit the tone—with me to leave Atlanta, I sensed there was more depth of meaning than was spoken and I felt an attraction I knew could lead to heartache. I agreed to move to Jacksonville when Terri left.

He looked relieved, held both my hands, and said, "You will be greatly missed but you are making the right choice."

On my last work day, he did not come to the office; unusual, because he never missed work except for rare business travel. There was no goodbye and we never spoke again.

In the Fall of 1951, I traveled down U.S. Highway 1 and temporarily moved into my Aunt Jeannette's Jacksonville home. It was strange to return to the town I left in 1948 when our family moved to the farm and I was a high-school girl. I enrolled in Massey Business College (not really a college, a school for would-be secretaries), and found a job. Soon I moved to the home of an older woman who rented two of her bedrooms, breakfast provided, to working women. The location was near my work and the weekly cost of $18 was perfect. Massey taught me a new type of shorthand called Speed Writing and I improved my typing skills. I became the school's poster student and I have one of the vintage placards posted in city buses on which I rode to work. I always took a seat far from the placard because the advertising stayed up many months and the picture became decorated with blacked out teeth, horns, crossed eyes, and other artistic touches.

The husband-and-wife owners of The Cooper Press hired me to proofread, correct grammar and punctuation, and do some editing, another job for which I had no training. Ed Cooper was bossy and demanding of his wife, Vera, who tried to keep everything under control and running smoothly. They were nice people but the pressure of deadlines and the perfection Ed demanded kept everyone on edge much of the time, especially Vera who practically trembled if he spoke harshly to her. During one of Ed's tirades, I overheard Vera say, "I thought Jeanne was taking care of that," but I knew nothing of the sort; Vera knew Ed would not yell at me and she tried to pass the blame. When she returned from the composing room, I said, "If my work is not satisfactory, I quit." Vera responded "Please don't do that; I am so sorry, please stay." When I picked up my purse and moved closer to the door she said, "Please stay. I'll give you a raise." That was a magic word. I worked for the Coopers for six years and threatened three times to quit, receiving a raise each time.

Within a couple of weeks after arriving in Jacksonville, I went on a blind date with Ray Owens, ten years older, who was an inspector for Retail Credit, now Equifax, and before I realized it, he monopolized my life. He was clever enough to take me to see the visiting Russian Ballet, gallery openings, and concerts of the Jacksonville symphony orchestra while pretending he liked such events. I would eventually learn he liked science fiction, football, and fishing. Period. He tolerated in silence the events I preferred until he snared me in his net. Snared is accurate because I was not successful in breaking up the relationship. He was nice but not a happy person. He was moody, distressed each time I said I wanted to meet others, to date others, and he would beg me not to see anyone else.

When I tried to be firm in my resolve, more than once he threatened to kill himself. I began to feel responsible, guilty in not insisting he stay away from my door, which is where I would find him soon after he agreed to give me space to meet others. He would be in my driveway to take me to work; he would be at my workplace when I was leaving for home. I began carrying lunch to work because he often wanted to take me to lunch. He was so ever present, I had no chance to meet anyone else, and he simply wore me down with his neediness and his threats to kill himself if he couldn't marry me.

Six months after arriving in Jacksonville I gave in to his pleading to get married, knowing it was a mistake but thinking it might work out. I was nineteen, he was twenty-eight, and our different ideas about happiness and compatibility began showing up immediately. Two years after we married, he presented his plan for our future; work ten years and save all the money we could to purchase a fishing camp in central Florida where we would live out our days. He planned to fish and guide other fishers while I managed the bait and tackle shop and rented the boats. He thought it was perfect; I thought it was the worst idea I ever heard.

We lived in a pleasant little house in the Arlington section of Jacksonville, near the St. Johns River. I made my nest, decorated, planted flowers, made friends with the neighbors and settled into a bland routine of fishing and football, very little music or ballet. On occasional weekends we visited my family at the farm. For each visit, Ray checked out three science fiction books at the library. He secluded himself in a bedroom at the farm, reading except for appearing at mealtime. When I told him he offended my family by not visiting or talking with them, his response was, "I don't have anything to talk to them about; we have nothing in common." He continued to read in seclusion.

I tried to justify the situation because I knew about Ray's unhappy childhood, the father who was gassed in WWI, who returned a "wanderer," away most of Ray's life and known through occasional postcards, and less in appearances. The postcards stopped coming, the father's fate unknown, and Ray and his mother began living with various relatives. Ray said he knew they were taken in only because they were kin but no one wanted more mouths to feed during the tail end of the Great Depression. It was this deep sadness in Ray that kept me trying to be happy, trying to make a bad marriage into something tolerable. My enthusiasm for life decreased; my weight dropped to 103 pounds, and I knew I had to make a change. A big conflict was Ray's determination to have no children and my desire to have a family. I thought his sadness over his childhood would diminish with time and the purchase of a house, cars, a boat, and a growing savings account. We were not extravagant and we both had nice jobs. I expected the acquisition of these possessions would change his ideas about family life. It did not.

Four years passed, slowly, disconcertingly, and I became more and more certain the marriage would never work. I was bored with proofreading and bookkeeping; life looked like a dead end for me but it was blind happiness for Ray. I volunteered in the political campaign of Braily Odum, candidate for governor. He did not win and I was chagrinned when he took an appointment from the winner about whom he said terrible things during the campaign. When asked what job I would like to have I was surprised and disappointed to learn the reason many people did political volunteer work was to get a job on the "gravy train." I said, "No thanks."

I continued at The Cooper Press and told Ray I wanted a divorce; while we were young, we should find compatible partners. Our partnership would never work.

His response was "How can you not be happy? I'm happier than I have ever been." Then the bargaining began with "If you want to have a baby, let's have a baby; we will go to concerts;

I won't expect you to spend your Saturdays fishing," and anything else he thought I wanted to hear.

I had difficulty dealing with his sadness, his saying "You are my best foot forward; I don't know how I can live without you. Please just give me one year to prove I can make you happy, just a year."

And, once again his sorrow overcame my better judgment. I said I would stay a year but there would be no baby. I was still in a boring job and a doomed marriage.

Another political season arrived and a young businessman, president of the Florida Jaycees, named one of ten outstanding Young Floridians, challenged the entrenched sheriff, Rex Sweat, in office twenty-seven years. Jacksonville, crowded with sailors from JAX NAS and the base at Mayport, provided prostitution, gambling, and moonshine. The general feeling was no one could defeat Sheriff Sweat although a few tried over the years. The challenger, Al Cahill, had business success, leadership, new ideas, passion, and sincerity as alternatives to the old sheriff.

Television and newspaper accounts reported Cahill's plans to clean up corruption and I distributed his political pamphlets in my neighborhood. The general response was, "Cahill doesn't have a chance but I'm voting for him." He won the election in a huge upset, infuriating Sheriff Sweat. I had not met Al during the campaign but decided cleaning up crime had to be more exciting than proofreading and I sent a letter stating my interest in working for the department. I knew most of Sheriff Sweat's longtime office employees were resigning.

A call from the manager of Al's insurance agency indicated the agency staff would remain intact and Al would hire an executive secretary for the sheriff's office. She asked me to take the civil service exam, which I took, and afterward I was asked to come in for a personal interview. For the first time I met Al at that interview where I was offered the job of assistant to the sheriff. I gave my two weeks' notice at The Cooper Press and went from dull and boring work to exciting and amazing.

Due to the anger of the defeated sheriff, Al and his officers were not allowed in the office nor sworn in until midnight when the new term began but someone had to sign papers related to the jail population. Since I was unknown and therefore not hated by the outgoing sheriff, I was asked to come to a judge's chambers at noon for my swearing in as a deputy sheriff and sign papers indicating I was responsible for the jail population. I received a deputy badge bearing the number one and was told I was in charge of the jail and its inmates from noon until midnight when Cahill would be sworn in. That was heady stuff compared to proofreading at The Cooper Press.

Less than a week into the job, while giving dictation, Al received an emergency call. He hung up and asked if I wanted to visit a crime scene. Of course, my answer was yes! We arrived at a droll little house, cluttered and dirty, blood on walls and floors in every room. A Jacksonville police officer had killed his wife and himself; the bodies were being removed as we arrived on the scene. This was the most dramatic event of my deputy sheriff job where there was never a dull day. In fact, I could hardly wait to get to work every morning.

My marriage did not improve. The determination I had not been able to muster came one hot and humid Saturday afternoon. As usual, I accompanied Ray on a fishing outing, routine except during football season. A typical Florida shower came from nowhere. Ray threw his old Army poncho over me with the instruction to "just put the fishing rod through the opening for the head and you can continue fishing." I sat on that Mayport jetty for a few minutes mulling a critical decision. I threw the fishing rod down, jerked the hot poncho off, tossed it aside.

"I am hot, bored, and going home," I said. "How long do you plan to fish?"

Ray replied, "Oh, until about dark."

"Fine. I'll be back for you at sunset."

As I drove toward Jacksonville with the Mayport jetties fading in the distance, I suddenly felt free, liberated, in more ways than one.

I resolved to give in to Ray's pleadings no more and start divorce proceedings. A phone call to attorney Perry Penland initiated the paperwork to close a chapter of my life fraught with disappointment. In a few months freedom would be mine for the first time in four years.

Chapter Six

Jacksonville, Alma Farm, Atlanta

Divorce in Florida, even non-contested, took months and Ray persuaded me to stay in the house; I moved into the guest room. He was a decent man and I wanted to make my departure as easy as possible for him. He had expectations of changing my mind by presenting a 'new' Ray. I knew I had moved on and there was no going back. Divorce papers were filed.

My work as assistant to the sheriff filled my time where every day was an adventure. Al's deputies arrested people involved in the numbers racket, moonshine, and prostitution. He discovered stacks of unserved civil warrants, some going back years, with the excuse "The person named on the warrant couldn't be found."

Sheriff Cahill responded, "I'll be dammed if that's so. I know some of them and can tell you exactly where they live. I want this backlog cleared up and if you truly can't find someone, see me and we will find the person if he or she is in Duval County."

Complaints poured into the office of Mayor Haden "Slim" Burns, who notified the governor, LeRoy Collins, that the sheriff arrested the mayor's friends and overstepped his bounds. In the beginning of Al's term, Mayor Burns suggested I visit his office to see how to keep records. There were 3x5 information cards color coded by race and ethnicity. Al rejected the suggestion and said we would make no distinction in our records. He further antagonized the mayor and city police department by hiring two black detectives, the first minority members in the sheriff's sworn officer department.

Efficient procedures and bidding protocols were established and required by all who wanted to do business with the department. Official vehicles were kept clean, employees were to be in a clean uniform or business attire. Al preferred his own tailored suits, never had a uniform made for himself, and he refused to carry a gun.

In later years, Jacksonville became a progressive city of lively restaurants, shops, hotels, skyscrapers, and a beautiful waterfront. It bears no resemblance to the town of the mid-fifties. The areas of East Bay, Main, and Forsyth Streets blocked the view of the St. Johns River rushing northward to the Atlantic Ocean at Mayport. The air floated a hint of beer, fish, and rotting wood of boat sheds and docks where an occasional fishing boat brought the day's catch for sale. This area of Bay Street contained numerous cheap restaurants and bars; places frequented by the legions of sailors on leave. Across the river lay South Jacksonville with a smattering of bars and restaurants in the outskirts called juke joints, some with moonshine and prostitution as added attractions.

A number of businesses appeared to operate with little scrutiny or interference by law enforcement. Mayor Burns considered whatever took place within city limits was his responsibility, handled by his police department. Former Sheriff Sweat left the city alone and claimed the balance of Duval County. Al came into this environment with a promise to clean up flourishing illegal businesses throughout the county, including those inside the city limits.

Records indicated the new jail, begun by the previous administration, didn't follow protocol. Purchase orders and other records revealed no bidding procedures were followed.

My uncle Jack Taylor, recently returned from Army service in Saipan, became manager of the department store that furnished linens for the jail. Bids were not required, monthly shipments arrived, and payments automatically made. The owner of the store asked Jack to check with his niece (me) to be sure the account would continue as it was. I told Jack bids would be necessary for all purchases by the sheriff's office. The account was moved to the low bidder; the store owner was not pleased and Uncle Jack never mentioned the matter again.

Al was confident as long as he kept his promise to the people and upheld the law, it was not important if Mayor Burns and a number of business owners did not like the new rules. Florida law, based in Spanish law, places the "High Sheriff" as the highest county office holder, above the mayor and the police department. There had been an understanding between the former sheriff and mayor that certain citizens were left alone, thus the unserved arrest warrants gathering dust and no-bid contracts.

New contracts went to the lowest bidder, unlawful businesses shut down, criminals arrested; complaints to the mayor continued, and through him to the governor. To insure all the sheriff's employees understood the rules, Al had a card placed at every phone and at the service desk reading: "Sheriff Cahill is here to fulfill the duties for which he was elected and to respond to the request of any citizen as long as it does not require him to break any law, or keep him from upholding his oath of office." We were instructed to read that card to everyone who called asking for a special favor; that ended most requests.

A television star, Professor Backward, asked to get his wife's speeding ticket "taken care of." I was instructed to tell the Professor that the sheriff would pay the ticket himself if it was a hardship but all tickets were accounted for and must be paid. That offer ended the discussion.

Al's refusal to bend rules, to break any law, and arrest those who did was great for tax payers but he created enemies throughout the city and county. Gamblers, moonshiners, and prostitution houses lost money. Friends of the mayor formerly could "do business with the sheriff," and they were determined to curb their losses. Mayor Burns was eager to help them; many were campaign contributors.

Thousands of young sailors roamed the streets, experienced freedom, money in their pockets, looking for a good time. These law-breaking business owners and the mayor looked forward to a return to previous fast and loose business practices.

Mayor Burns contacted Governor Leroy Collins to report Al created unrest among the citizens, intimidated the mayor's friends, and misused taxpayer funds. Collins responded by asking a grand jury be empaneled to investigate the charges. A parade of unsavory characters testified with complete immunity as to dealings with the sheriff. Al had never met most of them.

Some of these businesses previously hired off-duty deputies to keep order at bars and roadhouses. Al stopped the practice when undercover detectives revealed some deputies allowed illegal activities to continue and were looking out for the owner, not enforcing the law. Deputies benefiting from off-duty work were not happy to lose the extra pay.

Al was determined to tell the grand jury his account of events; he knew he had broken no laws, had nothing to hide, and wanted the lawlessness of his accusers to be revealed. He agreed to come before the grand jury but the rules suddenly changed; they would not grant him the immunity given to his accusers.

Perry Penland, Al's lawyer said, "I will not allow my client to come before you when his accusers could tell any falsehood with impunity. If two or more lie and will not be held accountable, the playing field is not level."

Al adamantly wanted to testify but his lawyer said he could step into a trap where all the accusers had immunity. While the accusations were ongoing, the governor's appointed auditors reported "All funds are accounted for and all transactions are in order." The grand jury soon returned a "No True Bill" indicating their findings revealed no wrongdoing. There was no basis for a case against Sheriff Cahill. The sheriff's department members breathed a sigh of relief; I was elated, believing it was all over. As the assistant to the sheriff, I knew he was honest, even turned down legitimate offers to pay off his small campaign debt at the Barnett Bank.

The celebration was premature. We were naïve about the economic impact resulting from upholding the law. The determination of the accusers was astounding. Soon after the grand jury's report clearing Sheriff Cahill of any wrongdoing, Governor Collins announced he was replacing him due to lack of confidence and unrest among the residents, a huge shock. The law-abiding citizens and many civic organizations were outspoken in their approval and admiration of steps taken by Sheriff Cahill. His attorney wanted to sue, to get the records of the accusers and prove they were false, but Al was disillusioned after what he had been through. If he stayed to fight the governor's unanticipated unfair action, a lawsuit would interfere with his ability to do his job. He knew he was honest, had done his best to correct unlawful situations, and was ready to step aside—let history speak for him. It appeared Attorney Penland had a strong case but the potential for making an even stronger case was a frame-up, not uncovered for years. A compelling reason to discontinue the fight was the inception of the relationship with me. He refused to provide an easy opportunity for scandalmongers to spread lies. Unfortunately, it would be decades before the existence of the frame-up to remove Cahill was uncovered.

I could not fathom Governor Collins' action until a chance meeting with Mark Nicolou in 2018, sixty years after the event, lead to the truth. Nicolou's job, entering Florida government-related documents onto the internet, led him to seek clarification about the removal of Sheriff Cahill in spite of a No True Bill from the grand jury and approval of all financial records by the governor's appointed auditor. Nicolou interviewed me as the Sheriff's former assistant, to fill in gaps that didn't make sense. The information I shared, along with voluminous scrapbooks, caused Nicolou to look deeper. What he found revealed Al was framed by three sheriff department employees, data never made public. I knew the men and was not surprised at Edgar Day, chief deputy, and John Shipman, but Wayne McClow's involvement was unfathomable until the rest of the story came to light. Sheriff Rex Sweat, became a wealthy man while in office and my belief is Day and Shipman expected more than a salary; there were opportunities. McClow failed to hold Shipman accountable for an alleged sexual assault which could cost him his job.

The report of licensed investigator, Mike Carswell, July 19, 1958 revealed McClow was compromised; he covered up the alleged sexual assault by John Shipman against Carrie Delores Lundy, a twenty-four-year-old married woman. The official report taken by detectives McCone and White is dated October 24, 1957. Shipman was not charged and the report was apparently buried by McClow to protect Shipman.

The frame-up reported by Carswell, involved state senator Tom Adams of Clay County, (the Senator representing Duval County refused to participate in ousting the sheriff) the Riverside Bank where a reported $10,000 changed hands, William H. Loftin, Gene Chastain, Joe Capps, and Hal Edwards. The plan, according to Carswell's report, was "to get rid of Cahill and hope that Governor Collins would appoint a sheriff favorable to them." Carswell concluded, "law enforcement in Duval County reached its highest peak of efficiency and integrity during the time Al Cahill was the sheriff." A former FBI agent, Dale Carson, was appointed sheriff by Governor Collins. It's unfortunate this cover-up did not come to light prior to Governor Collins' surprise action and the unfair questions it raised regarding Al's impeccable integrity.

With Al's departure, I was asked to stay and work in the department charged with serving warrants and other civil documents. I received calls from many outraged citizens who knew the truth and could not understand the strange action of the governor. I remained in the department a few months until my divorce was granted then gave notice and moved to the Alma farm.

I was elated to be with siblings who were preschoolers when I left for Berry, now middle and high schoolers. I had the luxury of not having to work since the divorce division of property was $10,000 cash—a considerable sum in 1957—Ray's old car, and a lake lot in central Florida, the area of Ray's planned fishing camp. I agreed to give Ray the house, everything in it, my new Chrysler New Yorker and $10,000. Complete irony; I sold Ray's "fishing camp lot" and lived on the proceeds without ever selling bait or renting a fishing boat. I left Florida with a suitcase and a couple of boxes. China, crystal and the sterling silver I began collecting in high school remained in the house.

The personal reason Al determined to get off the front page of the *Jacksonville Times Union* was the developing relationship between us. He protected my reputation and bore with dignity the "slings and arrows" from those determined to destroy him. From the day I abandoned the Army poncho, threw down the rod and reel, and saw the last of the Mayport jetties, I was a changed person. I did not have to do the bidding of others, did not have to save a flawed marriage, and it was not my job to save the needy person determined to keep me in his clutches.

Prior to Governor Collins' surprise action my office duties kept me busy and I had not been inside the jail under construction a block from the sheriff's office. Sheriff Cahill said he had to sign off on some installation and asked if I wanted to see the new jail. No electricity was on in the area we were allowed to enter and an open space was crossed on a long plank about ten inches wide. I hesitated because of my high heeled shoes.

"Let me go first and hold your hand to help you balance," he said.

It was a normal offer in the dimly lit area with exposed wiring below the board but I froze when he reached for my hand.

"It's okay. You aren't going to fall."

I wasn't afraid of falling off that plank but I was afraid of what I would feel when I took his hand. His touch sent an electrical charge through my body but I maintained my composure; Al made no comment as he helped me walk the plank. We made a quick tour and walked back to our office.

The next such feeling swept over me at the Firemen's Ball a month or so later. The sheriff's office employees bought a table where all could sit. Sheriff Cahill joined us explaining his wife, Frances, would come later. We danced with our spouses and with each other's spouses as was customary, considered good manners in that era. Frances had not arrived and Al asked me to dance. The instant he put his arm around my waist the electric charge was back. As we left the dance floor a deputy slipped a small handgun into Al's pocket.

"A member of the Chicago Traficanti mob in jail in Tampa put a contract on your life according to a letter the jailers intercepted," the deputy said. "We have undercover agents outside on watch and they will accompany you to your home."

Back at the table, Al said "Put this gun in your purse and bring it to the office on Monday."

He never carried a gun and returned that one to the detective department. This was during the period of "one more year to prove I can make you happy," from Ray. Frances came to the Ball but didn't want to stay and they left. She was not a friendly person, preferring their country club friends to the sheriff's staff.

Several days later Al asked me into his office, and as I sat with dictation pad in hand.

"You can put your pencil down," he said. "I want to ask you a personal question."

I had no idea what to expect. He knew I filed for divorce and I thought his question might pertain to that subject. A glass door and glass wall separated the sheriff's office from the area of numerous desks where public business was conducted. I was unprepared for his request in this very public space at 9 a.m. on a Monday.

"I don't know how to explain it but there is something happening between us," he said. "Would you let me kiss you? I can't get it out of my mind and one kiss might settle the question."

I looked directly into his eyes, hesitated about ten seconds, and answered, "Yes." Surprising myself by the ease with which I accepted his invitation to a kiss.

"I'll find a place for us to meet for lunch."

Al had been president of the Jacksonville Jaycees, Florida Jaycees, and had been on television as candidate and sheriff. He was the most recognizable man in town. His picture appeared in the Florida Times Union almost daily. Before the week was out, he asked to meet at noon the following day at a St. John's Apartments penthouse belonging to a friend. He would have the delicatessen prepare lunch and we could eat and be back in the office within the hour.

I arrived feeling like a high school girl on a first date. Al greeted me with a warm embrace, a restrained kiss, followed by a comment.

"That kiss didn't settle anything; it raises the question of where do we go from here."

The question was rhetorical; we both knew where we were headed. We talked over lunch, had another brief kiss, and returned to work. We were in parallel worlds: a budding love affair, more problems were anticipated in divorcing Frances who played her Catholic card, and the ruling from the governor hanging over everything.

I knew Frances on a limited social basis. Ray and I had been to dinner and football games on occasion with the Cahills where Frances talked negatively about Al in his presence.

"Al is not discriminating enough. You could put dirt on his plate and he would eat it."

She often sent food back to the kitchen even though it looked fine to my eyes. In a discussion of WWII, she said how much fun she and her girlfriends had at the Jacksonville Officers' Club during the time Al was a Navy medic assigned to Marines in the South Pacific. He was in harm's way landing on Japanese-held islands where sharp-shooters picked off the medical personnel to demoralize the troops. In three years, she wrote only two letters to Al. She didn't want "censors reading her mail." I disliked Frances but also felt sorry for her because she was discontented with her life.

She appeared to want sympathy from listeners while those who knew her were envious more than sympathetic.

She reluctantly gave up a job she liked when the veterans returned. The media promoted relinquishing jobs as patriotic—"give the jobs to the heroes who did so much." Frances simply was not the housewife type. She was active in the Catholic Woman's Club, spent her time at the Seminole Club and the Jacksonville Yacht Club. She had a maid to cook and clean, and bragged she didn't know how to turn on an iron or thread a needle. She entertained guests at the clubs, never at home, and bit her fingernails so severely, she ate with gloves on, slight traces of blood sometimes showed on white gloves.

Al told her he wanted a divorce, the tug-of-war began, and lasted nearly two years. He told her about his feelings for me and that I was divorced. She begged him not to move out but stay in another bedroom to protect her Catholic standing, rather phony since she violated the strongest rule of the church. She also asked him to go for counseling and he agreed. After several sessions, the counselor said, "for the first time in his long career," he recommended divorce.

Frances became more determined, said to Al, "That girl will never get anything, not a penny of your money." She spread the rumor, "A Georgia farm girl claims Al is the father of her unborn child and she is trying to force him to marry her."

I was twenty-five, weighed 103 pounds and clearly not pregnant. Not the profile of a poor farmer's 'girl' daughter trying to force a powerful man to marry against his will. I was suspicious of the frequent amount of time she spent with a married friend of Al, also a Catholic.

After months trying to reason with Frances—fifty-fifty division of property offered first, then 75—25, with his profitable insurance agency given to Frances' son from her previous marriage, to 100—0. After each offer, Frances waited the maximum time, sixty days, hoping Al would change his mind before she said no. Al stayed in a separate bedroom to let her save face, always hoping she would be reasonable.

One evening he told her he was going to the movie *South Pacific* if she wanted to come along. When the movie's Frenchman thought he had lost nurse Nellie Forbush, and he sang the beautiful song *This Nearly was Mine*, Al said he could not hold back the tears. It was his epiphany the way Mayport strengthened my resolve. He phoned the next day to say the only way he could get free was to give Frances every possession he had accumulated in seventeen years of marriage. He would be a poor man and it was unfair to me if he had nothing but a campaign debt of a few thousand dollars. I told him I never had a lot of money and I loved him, not money. I would happily marry him penniless. He moved to an apartment and the battle for a divorce increased.

Years after we married, Al told me just before seeing *South Pacific* he received a letter from my mother telling him I went out too often with Jiles Hamilton and he might lose me if he waited too long. I loved hearing she played cupid; I never let her know Al revealed her secret. He said that letter was on his mind as he listened to the poignant words of *This Nearly was Mine.*

He moved out of the house in spite of strong resistance from Frances.

During my months at the farm while Al lived in a Jacksonville apartment, he would often come to Alma on weekends. My family loved him and he loved them for their acceptance and their authentic farm lifestyle. His eagerness to join in the farm work impressed everyone, even cropping tobacco in the punishing August sun.

One Saturday there was a dance at the Alma VFW which we planned to attend after a hard day's work in the field. The men came in, showered, and Al said he would lie down for a few minutes before dressing for the 8 p.m. dance. At 7:30 p.m. I knocked on his door but got no response; he was sound asleep. Sweating all day in the field had knocked him out and I let him sleep. I left a note on his door and went to the dance with Mother, my siblings, their spouses or dates; the note was still on the door when we returned. Al looked sheepish when he came to breakfast; we just laughed. He was a pleasure to everyone; especially compared to Ray Owens with his ubiquitous books of science fiction, and his withdrawal to a bedroom to read all day.

I frequently visited cousins Terri and Elbert who had returned to Atlanta, as the saga of Al's divorce ground on. I enjoyed my freedom, dated old friends and participated in farm chores when in Alma. Al faced the choice of spending weeks in an expensive legal battle to clear his name in Florida, or accept an opportunity to help start a new insurance company in Atlanta. He chose the latter and moved before his divorce was final.

He took an apartment in the Druid Hills home of former Secretary of State, Ben Fortson, who became famous in 1947 by hiding the official Great Seal of Georgia when three men claimed they should be governor upon the death of Eugene

Talmadge. No one could be officially sworn in without the seal and it stayed hidden for weeks by Fortson until a judge ruled who among the three claimants was the legal governor. At the judge's ruling, Fortson, sitting in the courtroom, produced the seal from the Secretary of State's office from under the cushion of his wheelchair. He had been confined to a wheelchair following an automobile accident from decades earlier.

The missing seal was a big mystery for weeks with numerous interested parties searching high and low, locked boxes and bank vaults. There was great laughter in the packed courtroom when Fortson produced the seal where it was located in the center of the controversy the entire time. Al enjoyed being anonymous in Atlanta and exchanging political stories with Secretary Fortson.

Al wanted his family—mother, sister, and brother-in-law, Louie W. Strum, Jr.—to meet me. He phoned them to say he wanted to bring a friend to Lakehurst, N.J. where Lt. Commander Strum was the top officer in the Navy's Lighter Than Air program. They arranged housing for "the friend" at the Bachelor Officers Quarters and were taken aback to see a female at their door.

They made a quick recovery, surprised at news of an impending divorce, and gave me a warm welcome. They said they never really liked Frances for her treatment of Al during the war and afterward.

Before arriving in Lakehurst, we spent a memorable evening in Washington where we danced to Jane Morgan singing *Fascination*. The lyrics, "*Then I touched your hand and next moment I kissed you, fascination turned to love,*" was descriptive of our story and it became our song.

Al's work, hiring and training staff for the insurance company, began in summer, 1959, and TransAmerica Insurance was successfully launched in Atlanta. From the beginning, Al was the top salesman and began to rebuild his career in the insurance industry and pay off his remaining campaign debt. I visited with my cousin Terri in Atlanta as we waited anxiously for word of the divorce petition. After what seemed an eternity, Attorney Penland called to say Al was a free man. It was August 13, 1959; we were married the following day at First Christian Church, Decatur. The rector at the Episcopal Church of the Epiphany did not want to marry us due to our divorces and we did not want to wait while taking a required course for divorcees.

There was neither time nor money for a honeymoon but Al promised we would take a trip to Europe when conditions permitted. This proposed trip, a few years later, became a turning point in our lives and the lives of many others.

The weekend following marriage we drove to Alma for a reception on the lawn at the farm. The dress, made for my wedding, still hung in a closet. I wore it for the reception. We were the happiest couple imaginable as we began the adventure of fifty-five years of a good marriage.

Having children was of primary importance since neither of our previous marriages provided that option. Al was forty-seven and I would be twenty-seven two months after our wedding; advanced ages in 1959 for planning a first child. We were ecstatic when William arrived ten months later. We moved from a small apartment into a ten-room, French Normandy home on East Rock Springs Road designed by Leila Ross Wilburn, 1906, one of only two women licensed architects in Georgia at that time. Her existing homes in the Morningside and Midtown areas are sought after by today's house buyers.

Life for me was pure joy. I participated in numerous civic activities and volunteered at the High Museum of Art. The Museum's Women's Guild planned a June, 1962, trip for members to visit museums in Paris and other French locations. Al suggested we should take the trip and let it be the honeymoon we did not have. The tragedy that ravaged Atlanta's arts community was beyond imagining as excitement for the trip grew.

My youngest sisters, Lynda and Sandy, out of school for the summer, came for a visit. Lynda, fifteen, believed she was in love with Paul Davis and wanted to marry him. I thought I had two weeks to convince her otherwise and arranged for counseling. She didn't want to stay two weeks; Paul arrived after only one week, to take Sandy and Lynda back to Alma. In desperation, I concocted a way to "kidnap" Lynda by planning a Berry College Sunday picnic, told the girls how beautiful the school was—perhaps they would go to college there one day. I didn't speak truth when I said we could drive there from Atlanta, have a tour, enjoy our picnic, and get back in time to meet Paul in mid-afternoon. My guilt was compounded by a note I typed, addressed to Paul, and surreptitiously taped to the front door.

I wrote, "I want to stay another week and Jeanne will drive me back to Alma. Sorry I didn't let you know in time to save you a trip. Love, Lynda."

Next, I set my watch, Al's watch and the car clock back an hour as we began the trip. I privately told Al to drive slowly. I continued resetting the time when Lynda was not watching and when timepieces indicated noon—actually 3 p.m.—we found a spot at Victory Lake where we set up our picnic. After eating, we drove to Possum Trot Church for a tour and Lynda became suspicious about the time, said it looked later than the clock indicated.

I said, "It's overcast and it looks later but perhaps we should head home."

The Interstate didn't exist and as we drove through Cartersville on Highway 41, Lynda pointed to a clock on a store: 5 p.m.

"Gosh, my watch must have stopped," I said. "Al you better speed up; why don't you take the shortcut through Chamblee."

That was far out of the way to our house in Druid Hills. I wanted to make sure we were late enough that Paul would have read the note and returned to Alma.

When we were in sight of our house, I saw Paul's truck in our driveway and I confessed the forged note, the turned back clocks; all because I tried to save Lynda from what I believed was a bad choice. I thought another week of counseling might convince her to get an education before marrying Paul. She was furious, Paul was mad, said he would not leave without her.

Suitcases were hastily tossed into the back of the truck and Lynda and Sandy departed. I would not see or hear from Lynda for three years. The scene with Paul was bad but it was not the real tragedy; something far worse happened that day.

During the drive to Rome, we were listening to WSB radio when the program was interrupted. The announcer said the plane carrying the members of the High Museum had crashed on takeoff at Orly Airport in Paris, killing all passengers aboard except two flight attendants seated in the tail section. The date was June 3, 1962, ten days before William's second birthday. At that moment, I realized if Nelson Amos had not cheated us, we would have been on that plane, William would be an orphan, and my mother would have a toddler to raise.

During the halcyon days early in our marriage, Al received a call from Nelson Amos, a Jacksonville acquaintance, hospitalized following an attempted suicide after losing his money in construction of a commercial building. Nelson inquired about construction in Atlanta and Al invited him to stay with us and look into the market. I did not know Nelson but Al was concerned for his wife and four young children and wanted to help. Nelson arrived and stayed a few weeks in our home. He found a subdivision in Tucker, abandoned for years, with fourteen houses begun, none finished, on pretty lots around a small lake. He told Al he could complete the unfinished houses and there were ten more lots if enough money could be borrowed. Nelson's credit worthiness was gone; Al borrowed money from Tri-Cities Bank in East Point. Nelson quickly finished one house and moved his family up from Florida. Al was busy with training his insurance sales team and could not devote much time to the subdivision, renamed Lake Erin Estates. I agreed to do the bookkeeping from home where I could look after William, now a toddler.

Nelson hired workers and progress appeared to be going well. Each Friday morning, he called with the roster of employees and their hours. He said most workers did not have bank accounts and preferred to be paid in cash. I did the math, got cash from the bank, listed information on the bank envelopes. I then drove out LaVista Road in mid-afternoon and delivered the envelopes containing cash to Nelson. He said if the workers got paid before 5 p.m., he'd get little work for the balance of the day and he put the envelopes in his pocket. William accompanied me and we returned home prior to any distribution. Nelson received a salary and lived free in the finished house. I paid all statements for material by the tenth of the month to get a 2 percent discount. I didn't doubt the veracity of information Nelson gave.

I continued volunteering at the museum; plans developed for the trip to France. We made a deposit to reserve two spaces. When time came to finish paying for the anticipated trip, I received a call from a supplier inquiring about an overdue bill. I said there was a mistake; I paid bills by the tenth to get the discount. He insisted statements were sent and we were three months in arrears. When asked what address he used, he gave a post office box in Tucker, the subdivision location. A rifle, tent, camouflage clothing, and hunting gear—costing hundreds of dollars in 1962—were charged to our business account. From an employee I also learned Nelson turned in names and hours for men who worked briefly, sometimes only one day, but whose names were kept on the payroll.

Al called Nelson to arrange to meet at Lake Erin the following morning to discuss the situation. Upon arrival at the subdivision, a few idle men were there, no sign of the Amos family. The house stood empty. Neighbors reported a moving van arrived in the evening, loaded hastily through the night, and by morning, the occupants had disappeared; no word left indicating where the family went.

Stunned by this man whose life Al literally saved, we wondered why Nelson would throw away an opportunity to rebuild his career. We never received an answer, never heard from him again. I have received a few email messages over the years from one of the Amos sons but I did not follow up with him. Perhaps if he contacts me again, I will let him know his father unknowingly saved our lives.

When I bemoaned the 1962 Paris trip we would cancel, Al's comment was typical.

"Hell, we'll go on the trip, have fun, and figure out our problems when we return."

My response was also typical.

"There is no way I can have fun wondering how big our financial problem is. We are not going."

An accountant/lawyer was hired; the news was bad and he recommended filing for bankruptcy. Al said that was not an option; he would pay the debt if it took ten years. Lake Erin Estates was turned over to the Tri-Cities Bank and payments on the loan began.

I knew I could not stay home and have Al carry the entire financial burden. After giving up everything to obtain a divorce, he would have to start over once more with a big debt of Nelson's making. Without telling Al my plan, (I knew he would object) I found daycare for William and got a job at the Atlanta Journal/Constitution in the two-person industrial news department. My job was writing six stories weekly about advertisers' new products, new building, improved services—whatever we could make into a short story—and do the layout for four pages once a week. My resume for the job was exceedingly thin but I followed a lazy person who was years behind with filing. Within two weeks the filing was complete and I had my stories written for the month. The big negative was leaving a crying William at daycare. I convinced Al to drop him off; I couldn't stand to hear him cry as I departed. Luckily, we soon found Alix, a marvelous German live-in; she is still our friend sixty-plus years later. Alix Frank came to stay with us, William adored her, and I could go to work without leaving a crying toddler. Writing this, I realize it was the first set of events that let two-year-old William feel abandoned for a short period.

I became pregnant in 1962. Before my first obstetric appointment, I developed a rash. Measles in women is a problematic disease, especially to a forming fetus. The obstetrician sent me to William's pediatrician, who thought it was echo virus, not measles. That guess did little to allay my fears. The third month into the pregnancy, fate intervened on a Sunday afternoon. Al and I were at a movie theater. Minutes before the movie ended, sudden severe cramps nearly doubled me over. I wanted to get out immediately but we were not seated on the aisle. I whispered to Al I had a problem and must leave as soon as possible. I told him to walk rapidly behind me when we reached the aisle and not slow down to ask me anything. I believe the rash somehow damaged the fetus and Mother Nature responded. I felt a widening circle of red spreading over the skirt of my best suit but clothing was no concern at that moment. I knew my designer pale green wool suit was doomed to the trash can.

On the way to the car, a frightened Al wanted to take me to the hospital, but I refused. I wanted to go home and see two-year-old William; I thought of the possibility of dying and I wanted to be with those I loved most, not in an emergency room. Obviously, I did not die; I was having a spontaneous abortion and, over the phone, Al told my doctor I refused to go to the hospital or leave the house. The cramps continued and during the night, the fetus aborted; Al followed the doctor's instruction to save all relevant material; bringing me and "it" to his office at 9 a.m. Al gamely placed a plastic bag in our refrigerator. It contained a bit of jelly-fish-like material with a few tiny pinkish dots. Next morning the doctor examined me, ordered a week of bedrest and pregnancy postponed for at least a year to give my body time to regain strength.

After a year of protected sex, another year passed and we began to think William would be an only child; after all, I was already thirty-one. We were filled with joy when Carol was born two months before William's fourth birthday. I breast-fed her, as I had for William when Al began a welcome ritual.

"I can't help with the 4 a.m. feeding," he said. "but I will make breakfast and you can sleep in."

That began a routine lasting half a century. I saw no reason to remind him I was no longer breastfeeding babies. One morning when Carol was four months old, I went to breakfast slightly nauseated, felt it was from something I ate. Next morning, nausea more intense, I walked into the kitchen and made an announcement.

"I am pregnant. I have been through such nausea and I am certain a baby is on the way."

So much for the effectiveness of a 1964 diaphragm and spermicide. We were thrilled and excited to welcome Cary. "Two babies, totally different schedules; twins the hard way," friends said. We would not have changed a thing; Carol was thirteen months old. Cary was the sweetest, most loving curly haired child. If you sat down, before you realized it, he was in your lap.

My work at the newspaper, began in early 1962, continued through the miscarriage and Carol's birth with reduced hours in office and writing at home. My plan to stop work met with a counter-offer.

"A courier will bring work to your home and return for the finished stories. You can come to the composing room a couple of hours per week to supervise layout of the industrial pages and file your stories. You will receive your regular salary."

It was an offer I couldn't refuse, and for almost a year, I followed that schedule. Upon discovery of this new pregnancy, I told my bosses no amount of coercion could keep me, that I would be a distracted worker. I had a preschooler, a thirteen-month-old, and a new baby coming; no time for anything else even with Al's good help.

Our dear friend and helper, Alix Frank, returned to Germany to close the Munich law office of her father, Dr. Bosch, at his death following his internment release for refusing to join the Nazis. Alix, fourteen, and her brother, twelve, were forced to join Hitler's army. She anticipated returning to the U.S., but her mother's health failed and she never came back.

In the early 1960s, the newspaper was an exciting workplace. I was taking dictation when my boss, Hobe Franks, got an AP report and immediately told the composing room foreman to "Stop the press, Kennedy is shot." First time I heard "Stop the press." Fifty papers with the headline *President Shot in Dallas* came off the press before "stop the press" sounded again to change the headline to announce the death. I left the office with one of the fifty papers as people on the street offered $5, then $10, for my copy. I still have it. The scene was surreal; the familiar cacophony present in every department suddenly faded except the composing room and silence permeated the offices. In the streets of Atlanta people were crying, hugging each other in disbelief. I phoned the news to Al and immediately drove home. For three days, everyone I knew sat staring at their TV, transfixed as the shocking, heart-breaking drama, played out in Dallas and Washington. We didn't shop, or visit, or cook or clean. We cried and held our loved ones. We remember where we were when the news broke on November 11, 1963.

Back view of Jeanne in the backyard at Dixie Union at the age of three years and five months. Her curls were induced by wrapping her hair around rag strips for curlers.

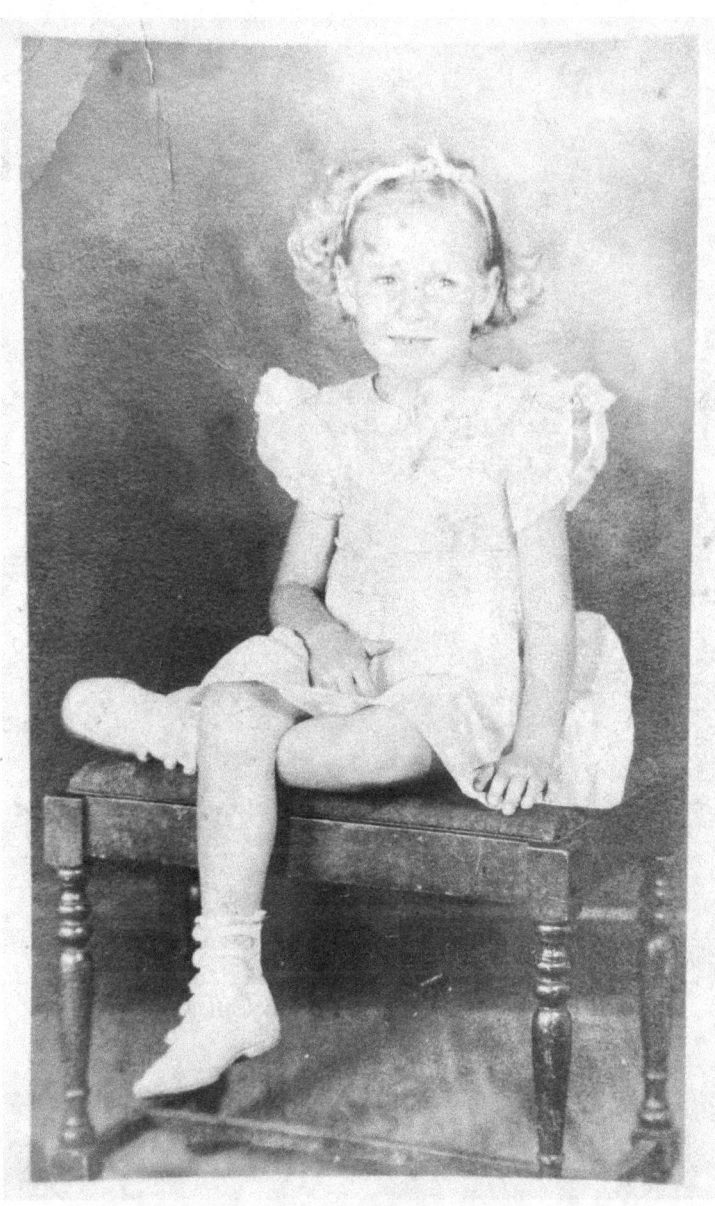

Norma Jeanne Taylor, 1937.

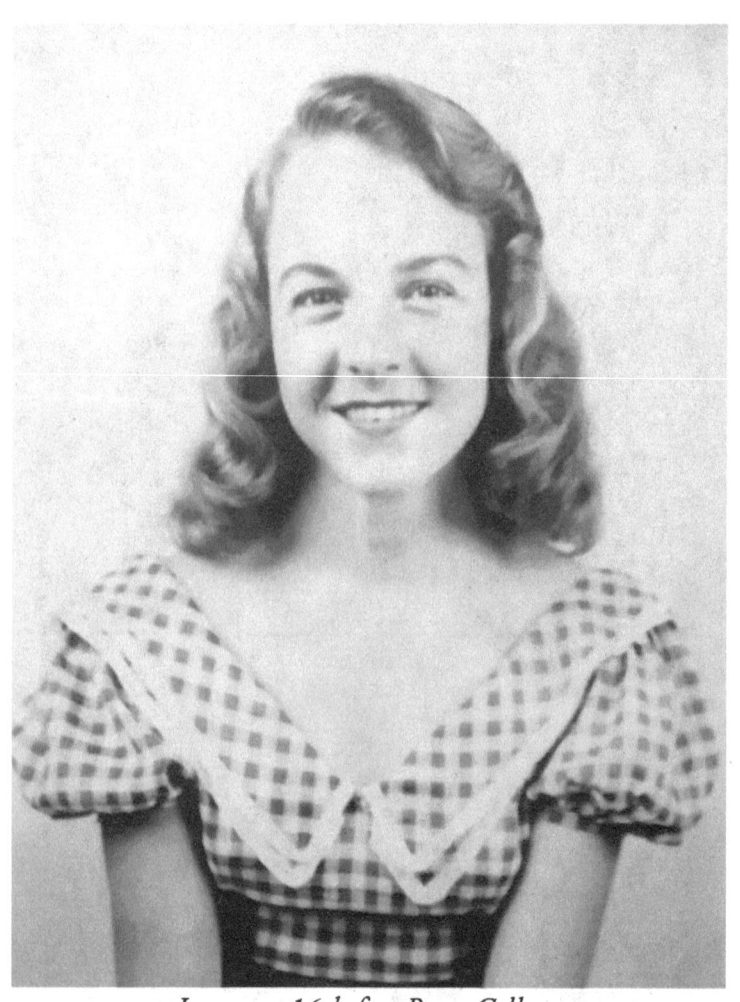

Jeanne at 16, before Berry College.

Jeanne Cahill, 1959.

Carol, Al, Cary, Jeanne and William Cahill in Boston, MA in July, 1972.

Jimmy and Rosalynn Carter, 1983.

Chapter Seven

Motherhood and Missteps

A month before Cary's May birth, we moved from East Rock Springs Road and the charming French Normandy house located too near the busy road. Next stop: Ivey Road, in Buckhead to a large home far from the street on a wooded acre. William entered the Montessori Early Learning Center. When he was six, we enrolled him in Sarah Smith first grade where he learned to hate school. Our decision was one of many mistakes of judgment. We were committed to supporting a strong public school system, felt it was the right thing, believing it would "work out" for William.

We were misguided as we continued down that path, learning nothing from the mistakes we continued making. All three of my children deserve an apology from me for not understanding them and their individual needs, for thinking everything would magically be all right with time. In the era of Dr. Spock, other child rearing authorities, I never heard the words "intentional living" or "unschooling." My five-year-old great-grandson was living proof of the advantages of today's newer ways of child rearing.

An important lost opportunity occurred as our first child thought he lost his special place due to the birth of his sister. Instead of just asking to toss her out he tried reasoning to regain what he felt he lost. He approached his problem like an attorney building his case, amazing logic from a child four years and two months old.

"Can we trade her for a seeing eye dog? A baby can't do anything but cry. If I go blind when I am old, a dog could help me walk."

William had sat for half an hour on the outside steps leading to the back yard, elbows on knees, hands cupping his serious little face. He entered the kitchen, sadly pleading as he posed the question of ridding the house of his baby sister, an interloper named Carol. Before her birth, Dr. Perry warned about this possibility; four years of undivided attention from two doting parents was tough to give up.

I naively thought we would have no problem; there was a calendar with each day crossed off, stories read, and girl and boy baby pictures discussed. Happy anticipation reigned supreme for a short time. William was allowed to get a puppy and he selected the name. He chose Gesundheit, a word learned from Alix, with runner-up name, Happy Herman, after a delicatessen. His primary concern was not appropriately addressed. I looked on his thought process as a clever and funny little story instead of seeing the seriousness of his worry.

Relationships between William and his siblings appeared fragile in the early years; an undercurrent of resentment increased during adolescence and teen years. I failed William at the moment he wanted to exchange the baby for a seeing eye dog. I didn't think it was serious, believed in time he would enjoy having a little sister. I should have reassured him of his important place instead of saying he would learn to love his sister.

Child "experts" reported the very young child could learn to read. Years before Carol was born our house was papered with identifying words stuck to the stove, sink, door, rug—almost everything with a short name—and, as we read the newspaper, William correctly identified numerous words and pictures.

Well intentioned, this probably added to his boredom when he entered first grade.

The move to 3620 Ivy Road in Buckhead occurred on Carol's first birthday; Cary was born the following month, May, 1965. There were children living nearby, and William liked Montessori; a big mistake was our moving him to public school when he entered first grade. We believed strongly in supporting public education but William was bored and hated school for twelve years. In second grade, he tested at the fifth-grade level in reading and comprehension.

He did not like school and we didn't comprehend how bored he was nor did we know how to help. We enrolled William in various team sports which he disliked even more than school. When William was twelve, Dr. Sidney Janus, psychologist, tested him and found his IQ was above 140. We didn't comprehend our responsibility to aid in the development of a special child.

He said he wanted to do sports where the outcome depended on him, not on a group. True to his word, his later sports became biking, kayaking, caving, and climbing.

William was fearless. He came close to drowning in a cave when water filled a section with low headroom. He thought he couldn't hold his breath any longer when he literally saw "the light at the end of the tunnel" and managed to swim to a spot where he could get his nose above water. Another frightful accident occurred in North Carolina when he stepped on a snowstorm-covered limb obscuring a small crevasse and fell about twenty feet onto rock, cutting his side with a hunting knife tucked into his pants. He was unconscious and his two camper friends took him to Murphy, N.C., where it was determined he had a concussion, broken ribs, and lungs in danger of collapse. Attempts to notify us failed for two days while he was hospitalized.

The same snowstorm trapped us at Big Canoe where Security took us down the mountain to the cottage of our friends,

Hal and Dorothy Gibson, who were also stuck until the weather changed. We played bridge, drank scotch and slept on pallets in front of their fireplace, the only heat. The Murphy, N.C. hospital could not reach us in Atlanta or Big Canoe; cell phones had not been invented. Eventually, the hospital called Big Canoe security with the report and Al immediately left for North Carolina to bring William home. The broken ribs caused great pain and the head injury left him light sensitive.

In his mid-twenties, William became seriously ill. An Emory oncology team diagnosed stage 4-B Hodgkin's lymphoma. Months of an experimental chemotherapy cocktail, bone marrow transplant, and radiation ravaged his body but brought no cure. After numerous invasive treatments he was sent home with a dire message from the oncologist: "We have probably killed him with the treatments. It will take time for his organs to fail." That was in the 1990s. In spite of seeing many doctors, he has never been given a diagnosis.

He and I went to our weekend home in Mount Airy, Habersham County, to decide what was next. He began a regimen of walnut hull tincture, wormwood artemisia, and fresh whole cloves. We walked in the national forest where he could go a short distance, then rest. Gradually he regained limited strength but radiation damaged his lungs. Extreme treatments kept him alive and for a time he returned to sports in a limited way. Scar tissue in his lungs gradually became more of a problem and it appears he may now have ME/CFS for which there is no effective cure or treatment.

William was not the first of our children to have a serious health issue. In 1965, we took them on an extended vacation trip around Florida. We made our return up U.S. Highway 1, visited attractions along the way and stopped at Marineland. Carol had fallen asleep, was grumpy, and didn't want to see dolphins. She and I waited in a small infirmary room where she threw up, causing me to think lunch in Daytona must not have agreed with her. She fell asleep and after the dolphin show,

we continued on to St. Augustine. Al and the boys visited Fort
Matanzas. I waited in the car with sleeping Carol. Last stop was
Jacksonville. It was 4:30 p.m. when we reached the motel and I
realized Carol had something more than an upset stomach; her
skin had a strange pallor. Al called a pediatrician friend who
came immediately to the motel. After a brief examination,
he phoned St. Johns Baptist Hospital to prepare an isolation
room and a spinal tap; he had a suspected case of meningitis.

The report was bacterial meningitis. The boys would not be
given antibiotics but would be watched. I was not allowed to
enter Carol's room; if I did, I would have to stay in that room
until the disease ran its course and I showed no sign of being
infected. I stood in the hall outside her room which had a tiny
window where she saw my face. Someone brought me a chair
to sit on during the brief minutes Carol slept. For nearly three
days her temperature stayed at 105°F and doctors worried
about brain damage; I did not leave the hospital until the fever
broke. In the middle of night, I went to the motel to shower
and sleep for a couple of hours. William's seventh birthday
occurred that week; there was no celebration. I was too worried
over Carol's life to think clearly about anything else. At the end
of a horrendous week her temperature dropped to a normal
level and she was released.

Crossing the border into Georgia our car made a strange
sound; we stopped at a small-town garage. The problem was
simple but the necessary part was in Jacksonville, a two-hour
round trip away. My emotional tether was stretched almost to
breaking in the mid-June heat, wondering how to make our
weak child comfortable. We were at a small repair garage with
no air conditioning. What happened next reinforced my belief
in the goodness of strangers.

After dispatching a worker to get the distant part, the garage
owner pulled an oily rag from his hip pocket and wiped his
hands.

"My house isn't air conditioned but it's yonder at the end of this side street. My wife's there and she'll help you. There's a swing on the porch where you can put your little girl and a big yard for the boys," he said.

I couldn't stop my tears.

"I think you and the children can squeeze into my truck and I'll drive you there."

His words were more welcome than any speech I ever heard; his wife gave us cool water and assurance things would be all right. Next came something else unexpected and beautiful.

This man, eking out a living by the labor of his greasy, gnarled hands, wearing patched, stained coveralls left us in the care of his kind wife. Several minutes later he returned with a brown paper bag which he handed to Carol. Inside was a red-haired doll in a red and white striped pinafore, fat round cheeks, and a smile so big her eyes were tiny slits. No one can look at that doll without smiling; Carol smiled weakly—the first time in more than a week. I am sorry I don't remember the names of that kind and thoughtful couple. They tried to quell my fears. I think of them when I look at a wooden angel on my kitchen wall. The inscription reads, "Practice hospitality—thereby many have entertained angels unaware." It reminds me to be thoughtful and kind to strangers, just as we were once strangers in need in a 'foreign land'.

In Atlanta, I took Carol and her records to Dr. Perry and told him we were lucky; William and Cary did not have to take antibiotics because she didn't have meningococci.

"Lucky? You were lucky but not for that reason. The strain she had was less contagious but far more dangerous." He added, "This week we lost a child with bacterial meningitis, the type Carol had. Often it is too late by the time the patient is brought to the doctor. This disease mimics non-threatening childhood diseases and progresses rapidly."

Only then did I realize how close we came to losing her. The experience left me feeling vulnerable, unable to make something better by sheer force of will. For a year, Carol cried if I left the room, prompting Cary to join in. Climbing stairs with a baby on each hip was a regular cardio workout.

Sandy, my youngest sister, completed high school and came to stay with us while taking a secretarial course. What a relief to go to the grocery store without three children in tow. Sandy completed her course, returned to Alma, and married Jerry Taylor (same name, not related).

Upon her departure, I agreed to accept someone on the waiting list for the Crittenden Home for unwed mothers. I was familiar with the Home because my woman's club was involved. In the sixties, a single girl's reputation was ruined if word of a pregnancy became known. They were often sent out of town with such scenarios as boarding school or an elderly relative afraid to live alone, or for medical care not locally available. Crittenden Home in Chamblee stayed full; a long waiting list created a demand for temporary housing.

Over the next few years, we had more than thirty young women live in our home, for one or two months. None from Atlanta, they felt free to go with us to the park, St. Philip's Episcopal Cathedral, a friend's private swimming pool, and other places we took our children. Our agreement was, by the last month of pregnancy, Crittenden Home would make room for them. Twice the plan did not work. One guest's water broke at 2 a.m., and later another guest went into labor at midnight. A call reporting the water break to Crittenden's housemother indicated no available bed. The routine was that the housemother must call a nurse to call the doctor about proceeding. I said we could not wait that long; I will take the patient to the hospital myself.

"You can't do that. They don't use their real names and their file has to accompany them or they can't be checked in."

I waited fifteen agonizing minutes, put the patient in my car, and took her to Crawford Long Hospital where Crittenden babies were born. Same story at the hospital as I whispered the situation to a receptionist.

"You can't bring her without the proper paperwork and she must be accompanied by a nurse. We have no way of correctly identifying the patient."

"Fine," I said. "We are going to sit right here in this waiting room until someone figures out what to do before the baby arrives. We are not leaving."

The receptionist rushed out, returned soon with a doctor and nurse. The next near birth incident wasn't as dramatic; this time the housemother quickly arranged for a nurse to come to our home for the patient.

Al was a great role model; he helped entertain our children, assisted with meals and grocery shopping, and treated every pregnant guest with respect.

He said to me once, "These are nice girls. They got 'caught' because they are good people. Promiscuous ones know how to take care of themselves."

Sounds patronizing, but from an older man in the sixties, it was a progressive idea.

William had a different understanding. His second-grade teacher asked me how many children I had. When I said three, she replied, "That's odd. William said he had four big sisters and they are all pregnant."

When I explained, she was visibly relieved; probably thought something weird had happened at the Cahill home. The waiting list was growing shorter as stigma decreased and a few single women kept their babies. Only one of the young mothers staying with us opted to keep her baby. She said her life as a mother was difficult. She worked two jobs to support herself and her baby, leaving little time to be a mother.

Pressure was put on the mothers to give up their babies for adoption. They were not allowed to see or hold them; it was believed it would be easier to give up a baby that had not been seen, not held. Knowing how thrilled I was to be a mother, to hold that tiny miracle, my heart ached for any mother denied that thrill. With changing attitudes, more women/girls (ages fourteen to twenty-nine at our house) stayed in their family home and kept their babies. We decided it was time to stop housing the Crittenden women as the need decreased and our children needed our time.

The extra rooms did not stay empty. Mother's sister, Mary Agnes Rose, and her daughters, Janet and Iris, came to Atlanta and we invited them to stay with us. We were happy to have them but after a year they returned to Waycross. Soon those rooms would house Lynda and her two young daughters.

The early 70s were busy times: My exceptional energy and good health hit a snag. I sought three opinions and all agreed I needed a hysterectomy. I knew psychics, healers, others with special gifts, and decided to talk to a Presbyterian minister named Dr. Brown, (PhD) who reportedly performed psychic surgery. A call to his north Georgia home regarding my need for surgery netted a guarded conversation with scant information except his comment, "If you come Tuesday to the home I share with my wife, be prepared to stay overnight, there might be something I can do."

Al drove me to the address, a pleasant middle-class house in a neat neighborhood, no privacy fencing or heavy shrubbery; Dr. and Mrs. Brown invited us in. After a brief description of my problem, Dr. Brown told Al to return the next afternoon to take me home. Thus began an amazing experience.

Mrs. Brown, in nurse attire, took me to a small immaculate bedroom, helped me put on a hospital gown that generously overlapped, providing total modesty. She would be back after I had an hour rest. With a sinking feeling I observed there was no reading material, phone, radio, or TV, and a daytime nap for me was unheard of. I fell soundly asleep almost immediately (!), and after an hour she woke me and showed me to a room with an operating table on which I would first lie on my stomach wearing the hospital gown; Dr. Brown was seated nearby with eyes closed. Soon I heard Brown take deep breaths, stand up very straight. He seemed taller as he announced himself in a heavy Scottish brogue as Dr. McLeod, a diagnostician. He walked beside the table, eyes closed, hands moved through the air about eight to ten inches above my body, never touching me or the overlapping robe. After several minutes he said, "Now turn over so I can see the comelier side a'ye." He repeated the same hands in the air, never touching me, then announced his call for a surgeon.

With that, Brown sat back down, took deep breaths then approached the operating table, announced in a clipped British accent he was the surgeon called by McLeod. Mrs. Brown stood with her hands in the position of carrying a tray which she placed on an unseen table. I don't remember this 'doctor's' name but I will call him Jones. He stared a short while at my covered abdomen, nodded, and reached for an invisible instrument being held by 'nurse' Brown. This was repeated numerous times and once or twice he rapidly thrust his upturned palm toward the nurse to indicate she responded too slowly. Nearly an hour passed, Dr. Jones (Brown) went through a hand washing motion then returned to his chair for more deep breathing. Nurse Brown instructed me to remain prone while she prepared broth and Dr. Brown could come out of his trance within a few minutes to provide post-operative instructions. When he awoke, he advised me to not lift more than five pounds, no exercises for two weeks, and no driving for four weeks.

Dr. Brown felt my need for the operation was the result of "having a belly full of something I didn't like" and the condition would return if I did not deal with whatever caused the problem.

After several minutes, both Browns assisted me to a standing position, held onto me a few minutes, and walked me slowly to my room. I felt in need of support, glad to have someone on each side, got into bed and drank broth. It was 4 p.m. My entire body felt weak, different, and I dreaded a long evening with no company, nothing to read, hear, or watch. I was told not to get up alone but to ring the bell on the bedside table if I needed anything. I immediately fell asleep; still sleeping the following morning when Mrs. Brown brought a light breakfast. I was incredulous over sleeping through the afternoon and night and had to be awakened for breakfast.

Al came for me as planned and riding home I told him the amazing events I experienced. My symptoms totally vanished for nearly six years then the heavy bleeding returned. The Browns moved to Utah and I was unable to find them. In 1976 I had the standard surgery and was amazed at the similarity in the way my body felt after each of the two procedures. I could not come up with the answer to whatever I "had a belly full of" in order to deal with it. Dr. Brown was prescient.

Interest in politics increased with the Georgia gubernatorial race candidates. Al and I were impressed with the intelligence and work ethic of a young Georgia senator who wanted to be governor—Jimmy Carter. I had a neighborhood coffee for Rosalynn and later we invited Jimmy to speak to the Sarah Smith School PTA where Al and I were co-presidents. We helped with campaign tasks wherever we could be useful. Always frugal, the Carter staff was mainly volunteers. There were no yard signs and when I inquired about one, the answer was, "Could you please just make one?" Al made a great one out of logs.

Following Carter's win, I was appointed to the Georgia Commission on the Status of Women, (CSW). Dorothy Gibson and I wanted to be co-presidents but the Legislature's documents didn't allow it so we took turns being president. The previous commission "worked behind the scenes to affect change." We were totally involved activists and openly challenged the wrongs perpetrated against females. Our victories were numerous: artificial quotas ended for women attending medical and law schools, health checkups and job training for female prisoners, changed laws preventing women from obtaining credit without the required male co-signer, changed requirements for the treatment of rape victims, published and widely distributed pamphlets on changes in laws limiting women's ability to compete in business, eliminated pink and blue pamphlets in technical schools implying specific courses for males and females; and myriad issues helped many women who were the family bread winners.

The Commission was especially interested in the work of Atlanta Civil Rights Lawyer, Margie Pitts Hames, whose case, Doe v. Bolton, was handled as a companion case to Sarah Weddington's Roe V. Wade. The Supreme Court's decision of January 22, 1973 prompted a celebration in Margie's honor. Mother of two daughters, active in civil rights cases, I was saddened when she died at age sixty, due to a heart attack while driving. The Georgia woman listed as Mary Doe, to protect her privacy, years later recanted her story. She claimed she was talked into having the abortion. On her deathbed she revealed she was paid to change her story, to speak against legal abortion. She regretted her actions and wanted to set the record straight before she died.

Sarah Weddington of Texas successfully argued the companion case, Roe v. Wade, establishing a woman's legal right to an abortion. From 1978-1981 she served as President Carter's Director of Political Affairs. Prior to her work at the White House, early in the push for equality, Sarah came to Georgia to speak in favor of passage of the Equal Rights Amendment (ERA).

We worked hard but were unsuccessful in having Georgia ratify the ERA. The Commission had enough pledged votes, scheduled to be voted first on the docket on a January Monday morning. Over the weekend Georgia had an ice- and snow-storm, preventing many legislators from getting to the state capitol and the vote was postponed for one week. During that interim, the paleoconservative Phyllis Schlafly came to town to a hastily called joint session of House and Senate in which she said the men of Georgia were the envy of women around the world because "You know how to treat your ladies." The halls of the Capitol were filled with people wearing STOP ERA buttons, spreading misinformation. i.e., mothers would be forced into the military, males and females would use the same bathroom, etc. The legislators and anti-rights members looked as though they would throw their shoulders out of position patting themselves on the back. Upon leaving the hearing room, one House member asked me: "How does it feel to have two years' work destroyed in thirty minutes."

Georgia had a poor history regarding women's rights. In 1920 it was the first state to vote against the nineteenth amendment granting women the right to vote. In 1970 while attempting to ratify the ERA, we discovered Georgia had never even voted to ratify women's suffrage. That oversight and slap at the importance of women was a disappointment; it was quickly added to the laws of the state. Georgia missed the opportunity to be the one state to put ERA over the top.

Missouri cast the winning vote in 1975.

The Legislature appropriated no money for work of the Commission. My dining room was the office, Emory law students and other student interns were critical to our work. Governor Carter gave $10,000 from his discretionary fund for printing and distributing *Rape and the Treatment of Rape Victims*. Copies went to every sheriff, police chief, middle- and high-school principal in Georgia. Word spread and requests for copies came from most states and a few foreign countries. We were pleased to see real progress as laws and protocols changed on behalf of women and girls. One small extremely important change was only a female photographer be engaged to photograph physical evidence of injury to a rape victim. Prior to that change, many victims withdrew from pressing charges rather than submit to the humiliation of police department male photographers recording evidence of injury to private parts of the body.

Upon writing for, and receiving a first-of-its-kind grant from the Federal Labor Department, I was asked to address a national conference in Washington regarding ways to tap into governmental agencies for financial help. Following the conference, I was told by labor department officials I should ask for a large grant the following year, due to the Commission's successful endeavors with inadequate funds. Sadly, that was not to be.

Jimmy Carter was completing his term as governor and it was traditional to offer to resign as his appointees, which our Commission members did. To the incoming governor, George Busby, I emphasized the Labor Department's offer of a significant grant, the need for continuity, and my willingness to assist new appointees in applying for a grant. Months passed without any response, no new appointees, and no one asked about the procedure for obtaining the grant, critical because the Georgia Legislature still appropriated no funds for the CSW. Women, girls and families in Georgia were the losers while months went by before any members were appointed. Unbelievably, the available grant was not applied for, more evidence the primarily male legislature had scant respect for women's issues.

My parallel life of mother, homemaker, and activist continued. We went to the Alma farm for Sandy's wedding and saw Lynda for the first time since the day I tried to keep her from an unwise marriage by "kidnapping" her. I knew something was wrong when I learned she and her two baby girls had been with Mother for several days. It was not the first time she had taken refuge from her husband. I asked Lynda to come with us to Atlanta. We were staying overnight at a motel in Alma but would return to the farm next morning to say goodbye.

I said, "If you want to get away from a bad situation, have your bags packed and you and your daughters can begin a new life tomorrow morning."

She was hesitant, "I'm afraid Paul might do something to Mother if he finds we've left."

Al said to her, "I'll beat the hell out of him if he touches anyone or even talks ugly and I'll see to it he goes to jail." Al doesn't look for a fight but when he makes such a promise, no one dares put it to the test.

I was afraid Lynda would not have the courage to make the change but next morning she quickly put me at ease.

"My bags are packed; the girls and I are ready to go."

Those words were what I hoped for and I saw relief in Lynda's face. Her beautiful blond, blue-eyed girls, Paula and Karen, were ready to go although they had never, before that weekend, seen the Cahill family.

Our "family" now consisted of three adults, a six-year-old, four-year old, a three-year-old, and two two-year-olds. This living arrangement lasted years and continued when we moved from Buckhead to Vinings.

We sold the Buckhead residence and moved to Orchard Knob Road on twenty-seven acres with two small lakes. We hired a Georgia Tech land planner to lay out a subdivision which we named Orchard Lake. The property had one existing large ranch house. The main floor had four bedrooms, two and a half baths, perfect for the Cahill tribe. The terrace level had two bedrooms, bath, kitchenette, and huge all-purpose room with a large glass wall opening to the lake– a private area for Lynda and her girls.

For the children's entertainment, we bought horses, Red and Rusty. Our first mistake was their purchase. The second was not realizing they would swim into the lake around the fencing extending several feet into the water. More than once, we had a midnight call from a neighbor reporting our horses were eating their landscaping. I wish we had a video of the capture! Al would put bridles on the horses, sit in the open trunk of my Cadillac as I drove slowly home. Al held the reins and the horses followed. The children enjoyed riding but eventually tired of it and we gave away the horses. Not many buyers were interested in our "hay burners," the name Al gave them.

Lynda took a secretarial job. She became assistant to three men building a new hospital, Urban Medical. After living with us for a couple of years, she moved with her girls to an apartment near our home. In time, she married Bob Green, who helped raise her daughters, and who is still the center of her life.

Work on Orchard Lake subdivision continued: streets paved, lot boundaries staked, and architect-designed homes constructed with wood and glass predominating. I assisted in landscape design and numerous tasks. I was especially interested in a huge shed built from timbers used in a building at the 1895 Cotton States Expo in what is now Piedmont Park and Atlanta Botanical Gardens. The 40 feet by 120 feet open shed — 17 feet high at the center, sloping to 13 feet at the eaves—with a dirt floor—sat in a wooded area near the lake. The heart pine beams running 120 feet lengthwise measured 16 inches by 16 inches and center-to-exterior eave beams were almost as massive. Karel Pruner, Cold War escapee from Czechoslovakia, degree in architecture from Oxford, dated Lynda. We hired him to turn the shed into a home.

Karel surpassed all expectations. To avoid a warehouse look, various floor levels were incorporated; a swimming pool was put inside with a glass wall and sliding door separating it from the living area. A massive fireplace divided the 40 feet by 40 feet area into living, dining, and kitchen, with a grill on the kitchen side. This large space had glass exterior walls with transoms above. The house was perfect.

In 1984, two years after establishing Advanced Fitness Systems a doctor knocked on the door and said he wanted to buy our house. Traffic between Vinings and Buckhead—partly due to the one-way bridge over the Chattahoochee River and two private schools with parents dropping students off—created problems. In a weak moment, we agreed to sell and move to a Buckhead condo near the store. I soon had seller's remorse; after all these years it never ended.

Al oversaw the building of five additional houses; remaining lots were sold to people who had their own contractors. The children were in school, and prior to starting AFS, I continued volunteering, especially political work. I even ran for a Cobb County seat in the Georgia legislature and came within a hair's breadth of unseating Ken Nix, an incumbent Republican lawyer. I was asked to go to New Hampshire as part of the Peanut Brigade for Jimmy Carter, an invitation too exciting to turn down. During the campaign, I went twice to New Hampshire, once to Ohio, Missouri, and various places in Georgia. Al went to Texas, Ohio, and Florida. We enjoyed the grand adventure at staggered times; one of us at home with the children. If I had stayed home and campaigned for myself, I might have been elected and had a much less interesting life.

Chapter Eight

Washington and Changing Plans

Many were surprised by the election of our friend, Jimmy Carter. Following a 1974 meeting with Carter insiders I believed he had a good chance. I was invited to the Governor's Mansion where Jimmy, Rosalynn, her secretary, Jody Powell, Gerald Rafshoon, Frank Moore, Jack Watson, and a few others listened to Hamilton Jordan laying out a plan. Arriving a few minutes late, I looked puzzled and Frank Moore whispered, "Hamilton is describing how we can elect Jimmy president." Soon after, Al and I began a great adventure, we talked with voters throughout the country about our friend, Jimmy Carter. I had no idea Carter's election would indirectly change me from homemaker to business owner by 1982.

My first out of state trip was to New Hampshire in the midst of record cold with ice covering every place one walked. Our bus from the airport transported us to our hotel where several reporters set up their cameras outdoors. I put on a big smile, gingerly stepped down from the bus and immediately found my feet slide away as I landed on my butt. The evening news showed the event with a comment about southerners learning to walk on ice. Immediately, we were put to work in the best organized political outreach I ever participated in. We received a map, a stack of 3x5 cards in order of addresses of registered Democrats, and a driver took us to the assigned area. After speaking to a resident, we checked boxes to indicate degree of interest and wrote any personal observance. Upon returning to the hotel, dinner was served only after canvassers wrote a thank you note to every person visited. That routine continued each day we were there with a successful outcome when Jimmy Carter later won New Hampshire. The Peanut Brigade fanned out across the USA telling those we met about Carter's successes as governor and his vision for the country.

Along with other members of the Peanut Brigade, our family attended the 1977 inauguration swearing in ceremony, a ball, several Embassy private parties, and a reception at the White House. The elegantly serene gardens and tea house of the Chinese Embassy were spectacular. The $12 million Iranian Embassy with ornate appointments and a huge white tent over the gardens was my favorite party location. A birthday party was underway for Ambassador Ardeshir Zahedi, considered one of the world's most eligible bachelors, (he was handsome, charming, and rich), host to movie stars and the rich and famous around the globe. The hedonistic, star-studded Iranian parties ended in 1979 when revolutionaries replaced the shah with a theocracy. The shuttered embassy remained abandoned.

On a later trip to Washington, I learned the United States park service mowed the grass and trimmed the shrubbery as it had for more than forty years. I was saddened by remembering the stunning effect of thousands of one inch mirror tiles, each set at a slight angle, covering the high domed ceiling of the Persian Room where one candle on a low center table reflected light from the tiles. Looking up was like staring into a galaxy with numberless stars packed together. I read the embassy interior was destroyed, the Caspian Sea caviar and Dom Perignon poured out. I cannot understand hatred that drove anyone to destroy sacred and/or beautiful places, property, or artifacts, and used religious beliefs to justify heinous acts.

Spectacular historic rooms of subdued beauty filled the White House, our treasured national residence, home of many

great leaders. In my opinion the Carters and Obamas dis-
played the finest qualities, the dignity appropriate for America's home. My three visits "behind the ropes" in the White
House during Carter's presidency increased my sense of awe
for the history made within those walls. Besides the thrill of
visiting the White House and embassies, our participation in
the Inaugural Balls was joy-filled in every way. William, sixteen,
elected not to go to Washington—as usual—Carol and Cary
enjoyed the festivities.

The chartered bus from our hotel to the Capitol for the
Inauguration provided a huge surprise. I was holding onto the
overhead strap, next to Atlanta banker, Dave Padgett, whose
wife, Dot, headed Peanut Brigade activities. Dave asked if I
knew Uri Geller and nodded in the direction of a young man
seated nearby.

I responded, "Oh, yes. I've watched him many times on
television. I want to meet him."

Dave said, "He's here escorting one of the Langford daughters and he does the weirdest things. Last night he entertained
us during dinner by mentally bending our spoons every time
we tried to get the soup to our mouth."

I grabbed Al's hand as we alighted from the bus and introduced him to Geller; Carol, Cary, and I, looked on as Geller
did the most amazing feat. Our brief memorable exchange
occurred with us standing on frozen snow, waiting for the
outdoor swearing in ceremony.

Geller asked, "Do you have something you want me to bend
with my mind? A souvenir?"

I had nothing "bendable" as I was empty-handed. Geller
demurred when Al proffered his Cadillac key. Al insisted he
had a spare. Geller took the key in his slender fingers and with
no apparent effort separated the hard steel key into two pieces.
He handed them to Al who remarked at the heat of the steel
in that frozen environment.

Geller said, "Don't you want me to put the key back together. Businesses are closed and you will be stuck if you don't find
your spare key."

Al said "The key is at the hotel; don't worry." We still have
the two pieces of the separated key taped to a piece of cardboard with the date and circumstances noted in Al's hand-
writing. It is impossible for a normal human to separate a
steel key with one's fingers regardless of strength. I would be
dubious if I had not witnessed it, surrounded by friends in
bright sunshine reflected from packed snow and the ease with
which Geller separated the hard steel.

Back at the hotel, Al found the spare key for Carol and
Cary who wanted to retrieve something from our car parked
in the garage under the building. Waiting for the elevator to
arrive, Cary dropped the key and it fell down the shaft. Al
and the children went with a technician to the bottom of the
shaft. The elevator removed from service—a large pile of trash
covered it—and the raking began. After several frustrating
minutes, our spare car key was retrieved. It was almost as if
Geller sensed something might befall our spare key when he
asked to put the separated key back together.

We returned to Atlanta and settled into our routines: the
children in school, Al's duties for the Vinings' Orchard Lake
subdivision, and my housewife/mother civic activities. A call
came from Peggy Rainwater, who, along with her sister, Betty,
worked in the Georgia governor's office and now worked in
Washington. She asked if I wanted a job in Washington but I
said that was out of the question; I had a husband and children
to take care of. Next, she asked if I were interested in serving on
a commission, to which I answered yes. A week later she called
with two commissions I might like—USO, or White House
Conference on Families; I chose the latter.

The next eighteen months involved hard work and the satisfaction of feeling much good was accomplished. I was not
prepared for the mean dirty tricks by a minority conservative

faction of outsiders trying to force their agenda on the majority.

Problems began before we commissioners were sworn in concerning the word "Families" in the name of the commission. Conservative groups, especially The Right to Life members, wanted only "the Family" accompanied by a statement indicating family meant a man, woman, and their children. Self-serving statements were presented on a variety of issues at dozens of state hearings and at each of the three geographically diverse conferences. We chose to take the conference to the people instead of doing everything in Washington. The first conference was held in Baltimore, then Minneapolis, ending in Los Angeles. The same conservative groups followed us across the nation, attempting to sway votes on numerous issues but failed to convince a majority of attendees at any location. Unethical methods were used but democracy prevailed and numerous worthy recommendations and research papers resulted.

An amusing encounter occurred in Baltimore where President Carter spoke, officially opening the Conference. Commissioners were seated in the front row and President Carter stepped down from the low stage, shook our hands and thanked members for serving. Instead of shaking my hand, he called my name, gave me a hug and quick kiss on the cheek and moved on down the line. I was immediately surrounded by reporters.

"How do you know the president? How long have you been acquainted? Do you live in Washington?" They were disappointed with my answer.

"My husband and I have been friends with Rosalynn and Jimmy since he was a senator in the Georgia General Assembly."

Reporters vanished, rushing to catch up with the president, hoping to find something scandalous.

Months later, work completed, our report turned in, I considered what we went through, including verbal abuse. I listened politely as one man shook his finger in my face.

"You Washington bureaucrats make me sick; coming out here telling us how to run our lives."

I saw nothing to be gained by saying I was an unpaid housewife from Atlanta; he preferred his own uninformed opinion. Even harder to hear were comments about ending government interference in the way families chose to discipline children and wives who did not obey their husbands. Same sex couples were subjected to ill-informed, ugly comments. On balance, fine research papers were presented, helpful suggestions made along with positive improvements in certain policies affecting families. It was an eye-opening experience, richly rewarding.

Most commissioners were distinguished citizens, committed to creating greater understanding between government policy and families. Coretta Scott King, Mario Cuomo, Steny Hoyer, Jim Guy Tucker, James A. Autry, Betty Caldwell, Ramona Carlin, and many other luminaries gave generously of their time and knowledge to improve government interaction with families. Research papers and volumes of testimony were submitted. With our work completed I began thinking about my future activities. I worked diligently as a volunteer at the national level for eighteen months and returning to volunteerism on the local level had less appeal than the thought of working for pay. I decided to get a job.

My first—and only—interview was with Delta Air Lines, conducted by an older white man who violated every rule in the book. He could see on my resume I chaired the Commission on the Status of Women and I knew what he was not permitted to ask.

He gave the usual, "You are overqualified for any position we might offer."

My response, "File clerk?"

"You wouldn't be satisfied with a position like that."

"You are right but I would accept such a position with the expectation Delta would realize I had more to offer and would promote from within when something more challenging came along."

"How does your husband feel about you going to work?"

"He would be quite pleased after my years of volunteer un-paid work."

"How do your children feel about their mother going out to work?"

"They are in high school with busy lives and would be glad for me to have a life of my own."

"Well, after your years of 'leisure' I doubt you would punch a time clock five days a week."

"I can do anything I feel is worthwhile and leads to a more suitable position."

Apparently, at that point he ran out of negatives and closed with, "We will call you if something comes up."

I was amazed to observe my interviewer's lack of knowledge about what was appropriate to ask in an interview and I was angry at his dismissive demeanor. I told Al I was not going through another humiliating interview. It was clear my volunteer work, no matter the level, did not count in that man's assessment of my capabilities. "I will just start my own business."

I asked my sister, Lynda, if she would like to work with me in establishing a delicatessen, that idea was soon abandoned in favor of opening a retail shop selling high end fitness equipment. Lynda and I believed that sounded better than cooking. The idea came from an acquaintance who had a plan but no capital and needed a partner to fund the operation. Al loaned me $50,000 for the startup of Advanced Fitness Systems (AFS) in 1982 on East Paces Ferry Road in the building previously housing the original Casual Corner.

CPA/lawyer, Fred Sheats, said, "Going into a business partnership is a bit like getting married. Both parties are in love but things often don't work as anticipated and you need an escape clause."

That was important advice and six months into the operation of Advanced Fitness Systems, I sensed my partner and I were not a good match. The agreement required me to offer my half of AFS to my partner and give him 90 days to come up with the money but I held the right cards. The accountant valued the business at $100,000 for the first year; $50,000 owed to Al. Jeff set our salaries at $35,000 and asked me to leave my salary in as operating capital since "you don't need the money." Jeff could not come up with the money to pay Al his $50,000, my back salary, and half the value of the business. His "friends who were ready to jump in" disappeared. He predicted I could not run the business and it would close within six months. His prediction wasn't groundless; I had no experience running any kind of business.

With Lynda's help, I took over as sole owner, April, 1983. Timing was fortunate, coincided as it did with a fitness craze beginning in California and progressing eastward. Al, Cary, William and Lynda helped me run AFS. Carol joined our crew when Georgia Pacific relocated to Atlanta. There were other employees but the family was integral to our success. The movie business was aborning and we had famous clients along with prominent locals who wanted personal gyms in their homes or hotel suites. These installations were chiefly handled by William. His greatest challenge was installing treadmills in nuclear submarines at Kings Bay on the Georgia coast. Partly disassembled, the units were still one inch too wide for the hatch; complete disassembly was required. William said it was eerie to spend hours reassembling the treadmills at the very bottom of the submarines in the narrow space between huge nuclear rockets.

William was good at his job, found creative ways to achieve results for difficult problems but a longstanding antagonism between him and his father remained near the surface. The seeds of this discontent, this seething, began in middle school and reached a near tragedy when William was attending Georgia State University and helping part-time at AFS. I came home from work and found a note from William saying he had gone to Laura's house a couple of miles away.

Al arrived after closing the store, asked about my car and was angry that permission had not been obtained by William before using the car.

He said, "Get your extra set of keys. We're going to get your car." On the way he said, "William needs to learn a lesson; you can't take something without asking the owner."

I was apprehensive but we were in The Father Knows Best era and I did not try to stop him, feeling his mind was set. On arrival at the girlfriend's home Al told me, "Get in your car, I'll be out in a minute."

He went into the house, returned soon and said, "I told William he could ride with one of us or walk home."

I waited a couple of minutes; William came out, got in my car, and began pounding his fists on the dashboard, saying "I hate him. I hate him. He humiliated me."

I tried calming him down to no avail, never learned what his father said inside the house. At home, he went directly to his room, slammed the door hard, didn't come down for dinner. He phoned a couple of guys I did not know who showed up, went to his room, and stayed quite late. Al decided to park my car out of sight at a friend's nearby house.

Next morning, Al left early to open the store and I cleaned the kitchen before dressing for work. William came downstairs, eyes red and dilated, teeth set in anger, and didn't respond to my suggestion about breakfast. It became obvious I would become the target of his humiliation and anger over whatever occurred at the friend's house. A few months later I tried to engage him in a conversation about what was said and why his hurt was directed toward me. I knew his rage was meant for his father but I was the easy target.

He said, "I have no memory of what you are talking about. You know I wouldn't do anything to hurt you."

I accept that was his truth; my recall of events is clear. I understood his pain, his embarrassment, which he refused to discuss. The important lesson is we sometimes cause the greatest pain to those we love most. For me, the answer that works is to forgive and love unconditionally.

William previously hitting his father at the store had roots in middle school and earlier. I don't know if it was Al's scout master or military training but his intentions were to teach a boy how to become a man. These episodes created a family wound with repercussions still felt more than forty years later. Writing this book was revelatory as the past was revisited. I was the first to fail William when he was four years old by not assuring him of his special place in the family instead of telling him he would like having a sister when she learned to walk and talk. Time and again he was the outsider, the one not carefully listened to as I gave words of comfort instead of expressing understanding.

I had pangs of guilt because I acquiesced when I felt Al didn't understand the kind of person William was, that he would never make him into a team player. Too late for William, I insisted on more understanding of Carol and Cary, what they might want instead of what he wanted to instill in them. The first time I heard him ridicule Cary, an inquisitive four-year-old with his hands in his pants, I strongly intervened and said "No more!" My outburst shocked him.

He apologized and had a better approach going forward with Carol and Cary. More than once, I asked him to step into another room, to remember our talk about child-rearing. It was another epiphany with no going back. He believed he was a loving parent doing his duty which was successful with Scouts and other youth but did not work with his own children. For William it was too little, too late.

Business was good, we continued to work hard six days a week but William had other jobs and no longer worked at AFS. We still went to Big Canoe on weekends, but something inside of me changed. William refused to talk about the difficulties and I blamed drugs and his feeling of impotency in trying to face up to what his father expected.

In 1992, Malcolm Menter, owner of Busybody, a chain of nearly thirty fitness stores in Texas and California, planned to enter the Atlanta market but sent word he did not want to compete with me. What a relief; he had moved into other markets, and with his buying power, undersold existing stores and owned the market. We came to an agreement and he asked me to stay on for two years as a paid consultant devoting ten hours a week in the store for the first year.

Malcolm later told me he had never bought an existing business, feared he would gain all the problems of a former owner and he wanted me available to address any argument or problem arising from an irate customer. Before year's end he said I didn't need to come to the store anymore because they never received a single complaint from any of my customers.

The ten years at AFS were fulfilling but small business retailing was hard work; required all hands on deck six days a week and no time to celebrate holidays. The house we owned at Big Canoe, an hour north of Atlanta, was our escape every Saturday when we locked the AFS door.

Three couples—our best friends—had weekend houses near ours and generally arrived at Big Canoe on Friday evening. Cocktails and dinner waited for us and we had wonderful times with Dorothy and Hal Gibson, Margaret and Dan Curtis, and Alice and Ed Steinmann. Saturday night and Sunday lunch usually saw all of us at one of these houses with great conversation, games, or cards. It was a huge loss when an aneurism took Hal, a retired Coca Cola executive, and our mortality began entering our thoughts. Within a few years Ed, who, in retirement played tennis almost every day, died of a heart attack, followed by Alice. Dorothy lived into her 90s, Al lived to 101. The Curtis's and I are soldiering along; I am the oldest remnant and in excellent health.

One by one, the houses in Big Canoe were sold but the happy years and great memories remained.

Margaret and Dan sold their Big Canoe home, and we sold our log cabin there in 1990. After selling AFS in 1992 we bought a large, historic house in Mount Airy, Habersham County, in the northeast Georgia Mountains. Ty Cobb lived there at the time he learned he had advanced cancer and dropped his plans to build his retirement home on a nearby mountain. The neighbors said lots of women and whiskey entered the house until his landlady asked him to move to a local motel.

After Cobb, the house was ill-treated with plywood walls dividing once gracious rooms into cramped bedrooms to create a personal care facility. That business failed before we bought the property and we began the task of restoring the aging Greek Revival to its former beauty.

One challenge involved a two-story fluted column. A rotten base allowed that corner of the huge house to slope downward and contractors were pessimistic about a repair. A Georgia Tech engineer/friend designed a genius fix that didn't require a crane or complicated scaffolding as others insisted must be used. A hinged steel belt, screws through holes matching the flutes, set within a steel frame held in place by threaded bolts at each corner was placed around the column's base. My job was to turn the corner bolts one turn of the screw each day. The column was lifted a fraction of an inch daily without a single piece of heavy equipment—not even a ladder or hammer—and the slow gradual lifting prevented cracks. Honey bees moved in but that's another story.

That ancient house contained unique features; the upstairs front windows had glass-paned shutters, something I've never seen on any other house. Bearing a bronze plaque designating historic value, owned by Senator Benjamin Harvey Hill following the Civil War, the house became an event destination called Seventh Heaven at 7th St. in tiny Mount Airy, Ga. A 2022 visit revealed the historic home designation was replaced by a small metal sign designating the controversial baseball player Ty Cobb lived there. No accounting for placing a good, albeit controversial, Georgia baseball player above a true Georgia leader.

The salvage and restoration of once lovely houses gave me great satisfaction and Mount Airy was no exception. Hours in the Habersham Courthouse revealed the original owner, a Savannah lawyer named Lawton, sold the house to Benjamin Harvey Hill, a distinguished Georgian who became a United States senator following the Civil War. Hill gave the house to his sister and her two daughters.

To escape the summer fevers, the wealthy along Georgia's coast sent their families by train to Mount Airy, the highest point on the rail line between New Orleans and New York. Another of the few stately homes still in existence was built by Dr. Sidney Lanier of Savannah, cousin of the Macon poet of the same name. Dr. Lanier treated tuberculosis patients and the second story of his home contained ten small bedrooms where he expected to house Savannah patients in the pristine mountain air. Just as the house was nearing completion, Dr. Lanier died of tuberculosis.

The hands-on work of restoring our house, plus a book club, civic association, and pottery-making lessons filled my hours. As work on our house was finished, Al announced Mount Airy was the most boring place he had ever seen and wanted to move back to Atlanta. I failed to recognize how few diversions were available for a retired man and I suggested finding a medium size town nearer Atlanta. The search brought us to Rome in 2002 where Al happily lived out his remaining years. His death at age 101 in 2014 left an emptiness, shared by all who knew him.

Fate brought me full circle, back to Rome where my unfinished education began at Berry College in 1949 when I was sixteen. In 2005, I enrolled as a full time Berry student, graduated with an English degree, and had the honor of representing my class of 2007 as valedictorian.

Fifty-eight years from matriculation to graduation is a record that may never be broken. I relished the learning, especially the literature and writing classes. That experience, coupled with strong encouragement from my youngest siblings, is responsible for creating this record of our family life before and after they were born.

When AFS was sold in 1992 and I began my so-called retirement, I thought I would read those great books, collected over the years, filling the shelves of bookcases throughout the house. I also thought I would make a beautiful quilt. The books are still unread and the fabric scraps given away years ago, not for lack of interest—I was just too busy. Keeping up a big house, often filled with relatives and friends before the COVID-19 pandemic, and my hillside yard with rock wall terraces sporting invasive ivy and weeds provided my exercise. The hours were rarely enough to get everything done but I was never idle, never bored. Gardening was therapy.

Many of us spent 2021 in our homes learning about supply chain problems. Ships and trucks unable to get goods into warehouses created shortages. Residential units were seriously affected. High demand for housing sent prices soaring and appealed to those with surplus real estate, or looking to downsize. I had a house and garden larger than I needed and I sold my home at #7 Lookout Avenue, plus a rental house at 515 S. Broad St. and a few residential lots. I planned to live with Carol in Hapeville which I did for a few months.

When I decided I needed my own kitchen, Carol found a house three blocks away from her home with commercial potential on Hapeville's N. Central Avenue. It appeared I was the only owner-occupant of a historic house left on this primary street in the heart of town. With a coffee shop/cafe on my left and a dry cleaner on the right, it wasn't a house most 90-year-old widows might choose but it had a spectacular view of planes lined up above the tree tops for runway approach at the world's busiest airport.

Hapeville's two and a half square mile footprint put almost everything in easy walking distance for me. I lived in the downstairs area and had two female tenants upstairs. One with Delta; the other went to New York temporarily studying acting, It was an ideal arrangement; I was not alone and the income was a plus.

My big decision was where I wanted to spend my final years. Recently, I mused about my situation, stated to a friend I thought I would die in a familiar home, surrounded by artifacts of my choosing, in the company of people I loved, and now I don't have that.

His response was, "If you had died ten years ago you would have had all of that."

Wow! How wise and welcome were those words. For starters, I would not have known my precious great grandchild who has given me happiness beyond measure. My attitude shifted from how little time I had left to how much joy life brought every day and how much activity could be fitted in.

I have not decided where I actually want to live out my remaining years but as Robert Frost wrote, I have "miles to go and promises to keep before I sleep." I have liked all the many places I called home and I expect that luck will follow me wherever I go. Opportunities and good people abound everywhere; there is no intense pressure to make a hasty decision. However, if I wait too long, life will make that decision for me.

Chapter Nine

Thorns Pierced the Bed of Roses

T he recitation of happy events described the good times, and there were many, but there was a dark underside I failed to recognize as the fabric unraveled. Al and I planned to join three couples, friends, for Delta's inaugural direct flight to London, April 30, 1978. We booked our trip through our friend and former Atlanta mayor, Sam Massell's travel agency. In London, we joined a small group Trafalgar Tour. From London we went to Paris, Brussels, Dresden, Amsterdam, Zurich, Innsbruck and Monaco. It was a grand trip and we arrived home on Cary's thirteenth birthday.

The evening that we walked into our house upon returning from Europe, I sensed something had changed, something was wrong. I was not prepared for the truth; people we knew and trusted betrayed that trust in a heartbreaking way. We had left our children in their care, believing they were safe. The pain for our family has decreased; it will never go away completely. We trusted unworthy people that fooled us with Jekyll and Hyde split personalities, cleverly hidden. The damage was done and I don't wish to have my children revisit the occurrence by detailing it here.

Along with many friends who were parents, we were also concerned over the presence of drugs available to teenagers and unsure about keeping our children safe. The 70s were turbulent with run-away kids on the streets in Atlanta's Piedmont Park area. The Northside Junior Woman's Club members volunteered to help paint the interior of a large home donated by a benefactor as a residence for runaway youth. Hand-me-down furniture was collected, young occupants moved in and the woman's club provided refreshments in celebration. Over-crowded from the beginning, I felt sorry for the residents squeezed onto the faded furniture, sitting in open spaces on the floor, poking their heads through the screenless window openings. They were having fun playing guitars, singing, and dancing on the porch.

Festivities aside, what I saw was too few beds, an ill-equipped kitchen, two small bathrooms for twelve or more residents and no actual onsite supervision. I called authorities about supervision; I was told city and county agencies were overseeing several locations and getting a handle on the burgeoning influx of young people and drugs. William and his high school friends were experimenting with drugs; resulting in frightened parents clueless about what to do.

I thought it would be a good idea to let Carol and Cary see what poor living conditions existed for runaways, expose the absence of comfort and lack of privacy experienced by the young residents of the group home. The three of us made sandwiches and cookies, packed water and juice, and called to schedule a visit. The visit went well, the house even more crowded, and a newcomer had a pet monkey. The visit was Exhibit A for a well-meaning parent, clueless about the impression made on ten- and eleven-year-olds. Years later Carol remembered the house as the coolest place, a house where she and Cary would love to reside.

William still hated the team sports Al insisted upon—and I was complicit, hoping Al knew best due to years of award-winning work with youth. I learned much later of a poorly handled situation that was right in front of me and I didn't "get" it. Eventually, William confided one reason he hated basketball and didn't like to be on the court was his cheap basketball

shoes when most players had Nike's and other popular shoes.
Not only were the shoes an embarrassment, he said we never
bought him a Gant shirt with the little loop on the back which
all the cool boys were wearing. I was oblivious to his feelings;
labels and "what everyone was wearing" were not important
to me. I am sorry for his humiliation that went unrecognized
and I don't remember he ever mentioned his concern until
adulthood. That was too late. He would have had Nikes and a
Gant shirt if I'd known of the embarrassment he felt.

Once, as we prepared to take the family to a basketball game,
William tried to beg off, saying he felt ill. Al slid his belt off,
gave a couple of hits, leaving evidence on William's legs, and
we went to the middle school gym for the game. At halftime
Al asked the coach why he had not put William in the game.
The coach said William told him he felt ill, and didn't feel like
playing.

Al replied, "He's not sick, send him in."

An embarrassed William joined the game with belt marks
lightly visible on his leg. He had to have been totally humiliated. It was near season's end and I told William we would never
sign him up for any more teams. I was devastated at my failure
to recognize the importance of having what his classmates were
wearing. He said he wanted to do sports where the outcome
was up to him, not dependent on the action of others. He
became a mountain biker, ice- and rock-climber, caver, and
kayaker. He was outstanding—and a good teacher—in each
of these sports. Al, a wonderful father most of the time, never
understood William's dislike and frustration of being forced
into team sports. Seeds of anger and rejection planted in middle school, or perhaps earlier as a four-year-old, suppressed for
years, bore bitter fruit.

I arranged for family counseling. The first meeting involved
all of us; the second, Al and I met with the counselor, and
the third was to be Al and the counselor. Al announced he
attended two sessions and would take no more time from his

work to talk; William was the one "who needed to be fixed." That ended family counseling but William withdrew more into himself and, although he kept up with school work, drugs were readily available to high schoolers and he was part of that scene.

William worked part-time at a friend's nearby Vinings restaurant now named Canoe, and later at another friend's business, Vinings Chemical Co. where chemical exposure might have been the genesis of his struggle years later with Hodgkin's lymphoma. He bought a small motorcycle which he rode to school. One afternoon, upon arriving home, he drove it right into a large tree in our yard and it was obvious he was high on some unknown substance.

Soon we took him to a psychiatrist who recommended he be enrolled in Peachford Hospital's two-week drug program for youth. Three or four days prior to completion of the course he escaped fifteen miles from home, and he phoned me to come get him. I agreed to come but only to return him to Peachford to finish the course. After minutes of pleading, he went back but said the program was no help. He continued to express lack of interest in family activities; turning down invitations to a private dinner with the Carters for our family at the governor's mansion, the inauguration in Washington, and vacations in Mexico, Hawaii, and Florida.

He never wanted to discuss these decisions. We failed him, not for lack of concern or love but we didn't know what to do and hoped he would "grow out of it." I didn't understand his needs until it was too late for the life he could have had, instead of the mold we attempted to force on him. His best memories of his father were learning to use tools and the skill gained in mechanical and carpentry projects.

Upon graduation, William wanted to go to the University of Georgia with friends but I had no confidence in his ability to avoid the party scene and drugs. We agreed to pay for Georgia State University for a year with him living at home. If successful, we would talk about a change to UGA. He enrolled at GSU, got a part-time job but disliked the lack of campus life and didn't make friends; most students were mature, rushing off to their own part-time jobs or home to their family. After the first semester he showed no further interest in college.

Meanwhile, Carol and her girlfriends were not hesitant to indulge in neighborhood mischief while Cary was the ideal child throughout his early teens. He got his learner's permit and began pressing his case for a car. I suggested finding a car in need of repair prior to his birthday. He could learn maintenance and be more careful if he was responsible for its condition.

That was another well-meaning, unheeded, unworkable idea as his sixteenth birthday approached.

After several hours of car shopping, Al and Cary returned with a baby-blue convertible in perfect condition. For Cary the car was love at first sight and Al couldn't say no. The freedom of a car, and the pressure of being a closeted homosexual—a fact I did not know until the AIDS epidemic arrived in the mid-80s—created a rift, years of heartache and a lack of understanding what he was going through.

Once, we almost had a conversation.

"I can't talk about what has changed ...

He got up from the table and started to walk out of the room, but turned back.

"I will tell you when I think you can handle it," he said.

I didn't press him; it was a missed opportunity to talk perhaps about his sexuality which he hid so well it was not even a part of my vocabulary.

The classy blue convertible, the May birthday gift, put him on top of the world and Al presented the rules. Cary would be allowed one ticket each for a list of minor traffic violations—speeding, parking, etc.— but anything more serious would mean the end of the car. In June, the car filled with friends, several rules were broken by driving on Daytona Beach attracting the authorities and resulting in numerous citations. Cary's call to his father, his only option to keep the fun lovers from being detained, resulted in Al doing whatever the officials required to let Cary drive back to Atlanta. The next day, Al sold the car and we never bought Cary another one. He was devastated but understood he was warned; Al kept his word.

Years later I tried to comprehend my unawareness of homosexuality and decided time and place played a role in my ignorance. The 1940s Georgia town of Alma, where I lived, would require one to have unimaginable courage to admit being gay and I never heard that word mentioned. During college in the Berry "bubble" the word gay never came up in my presence. In Atlanta, my date, Jerry Bennett, once stayed too late and missed the last trolley from Chamblee to Georgia Tech in downtown Atlanta and he caught a ride with a stranger. He told me the conversation was normal for the first few miles then he turned down an invitation to go home with the driver.

"I told him no, and then he dropped me off at my fraternity house where I thanked him for the ride and said 'I hope we both have better luck next time.'"

That brief exchange in no way prepared me to recognize my own son was a homosexual man. During the mid-eighties' HIV scare, Carol broke the news and my only thought was how difficult life would be for him, facing the ugliness, rejection, and outright hatred of too many people. I was shocked at my ignorance of his sexuality but felt only acceptance and love for Cary. There was never a thought of condemnation or any sort of shame.

I believed I failed him because I had not instilled enough confidence to share with me the secret he lived with for many troubled years. Nor did I recognize the harmful choices he made early in his personal affairs, resulting in pain and drug abuse leading to three suicide attempts over the years. He is caring and sympathetic toward friends and strangers, kittens and puppies, often to his own detriment.

I believed each of his attempts—to overcome difficulties, to make a new beginning—would be successful. I was too ready to accept the excuses, to be an enabler, to pay the electric bill so the heat would stay on. The pain I felt as I acknowledged my mistakes of judgment is palpable. I always believed he was too caring, too gentle for the times. He would give money to friends in need, knowing I would always come to his rescue. A mother's love is so overpowering it defies explanation. I have no words to describe the wrenching pain of looking into the blood-drained face of a loved one, as medical technicians struggle to get a heartbeat, a breath, any sign of life. I believed I had to do whatever I could to keep him alive until he found his way to the life that waited for him. I believed he was too sensitive and once again I didn't know how to help him. His efforts to help himself over and over failed. Fortunately, after a long struggle, he found the answers and became the happy person he was meant to be. He found a marvelous partner; his creative talents were recognized and his work allowed him to use those skills.

Our children experienced disappointments and heartaches on the journey to adulthood. My teenage expectation of being that perfect mother of perfect children was swept away in the tsunami called life. Instead, they are well rounded, accomplished individuals, involved in the world, conscious of their role in saving the planet and subservient to only themselves and those of their choosing.

Did I go wrong following the advice of Dr. Spock and other child experts? I gave unconditional love but could not prevent the pitfalls, the illnesses, the misunderstandings. We loved and accepted each other regardless of missteps. Enlightenment came decades later as I observed my granddaughter's interaction with my great-grandchild. There was no thought of "It's eleven-thirty, I must make lunch," or "the floor is cold, we must put on your shoes." Rather, lunch is made whenever hunger is expressed, and if the feet are cold, no problem, so what. The result is a happy, extremely resourceful child, allowed to make missteps and learn from the experience.

My children didn't have those opportunities to experience the consequences of poor decisions along the way. I realize my desire to give them a more organized life than I had was not what they needed. If I had let them learn to maneuver tiny stones in their youthful path, perhaps there would have been fewer boulders. I am sorry I took too long to learn how smoothing the way was not a path to happiness. I hope they forgave their well-intentioned mother for the many misunderstandings, omissions, and mistakes I made, not from lack of love, but from failing to acknowledge what they needed.

The isolation and resentment William felt when called upon to give up the exalted position of only child to parents who desperately wanted children was not appropriately addressed. I didn't recognize the seriousness of his desire to retain his position of being the special child for the formative first four years of his life. I believed it was a stage he would grow out of but that was a serious misunderstanding of the importance of his feeling of rejection. That pattern continued in his lack of closeness to his siblings and it pains me to realize the steps I failed to take all those years ago.

Al was a good father who believed it was his duty to fit William into a role; instead, he was a misunderstood outsider son who was never listened to. I accepted responsibility for not realizing or dealing with his deep-seated resentment. I am sorry I can't turn back time, to understand the critical needs of each of three precious babies entrusted to our care.

In spite of my missteps and lack of awareness, William, Carol, and Cary are thoughtful, considerate adults who actively participate in creating a better world for future generations. William's once strong body, ravaged by treatments to quell Stage 4B Hodgkins lymphoma—no longer able to perform his sports—pursued measures to create the smallest possible carbon footprint. He lived a solitary life in an old log cabin on farm acres growing rank in pine trees and weeds. I visited every week or ten days to grocery shop, did limited cooking, and offered help with whatever project he had in the works. He expressed concern for the future because I am the only person he felt was in his corner. At my age—ninety-two—he recognized how few years I have remaining. Friends from his days of strenuous sporting activities, also aged, gave up those pleasures, and stopped calling to see if William was up to some bouldering, or bicycling—old pursuits they also abandoned. He lived almost off-grid with captured rain water, solar panels, rocket stove, cob walls in his added green-house room, and whatever power innovation he learned from Scientific American, the reading material he followed with interest.

The "unkindest cut of all" was the discovery of advanced cancer debilitating his body. He was sent home after Emory doctors treated him with the latest tools at their disposal: chemo cocktail, bone marrow transplant, and radiation which created scar tissue in his lungs and resulted in breathing complications. His determination and lungs, strong from early activities, kept him alive but with a diminished quality of life. Upon releasing William, his oncology team did not expect more than a few months and were surprised to learn he was alive many years later.

It was painful to watch his loneliness and his struggle to breathe, to know his quality of life was gone. He endured numerous misdiagnoses before discovering what appeared to be myalgia encephalomyelitis and chronic fatigue syndrome (ME/CFS) for which there is no cure and no treatment according to CDC. The search continued in spite of such reports. After visits with him I drove away with barely controlled tears for William's lost future.

Carol was a winner by all measures. She was prescient in observing opportunities Hollywood was exporting to Atlanta via the burgeoning movie industry. She created a company listing rentable spaces for crew and cast. These contacts led to sales of property to those who wanted a more permanent home; and, she turned her private home into a multi-faceted, beautiful event location. Her talents were finding answers to questions and trends before others knew what to ask. Following the unfortunate events of her teen years she returned to Atlanta from Portland, worked at AFS part time, attended Georgia State University briefly, married Ray Bouley and had Kirk and Lady, the grandchildren that brought great joy to all our lives. The star on our family tree was the arrival of a great-grandchild to parents Ladybird and Emmett Woods in 2020.

Carol's popularity continued to grow with Hapeville's leaders as her ideas were instrumental in bringing studios for dozens of artists to town. This coup is the latest of several business accomplishments in Atlanta/Hapeville and beyond. Carol is the go-to person for Hapeville, the tiny town in the bosom of the world's busiest airport. She continued to think ahead and we have all benefited from her foresight.

Cary, a caring, thoughtful adult is an amazing artist, creative with carpentry tools and a blank slate before him. After much exploration, successes, and tragedies he has become the person, and found the life he wants and needs. The journey was challenging as he searched for a 'home' from Miami Beach to Cape Cod, the Hudson Valley and NYC, to places in between and even beyond the States. I wrote about some of the hills and valleys he experienced, and his unflagging determination to help others, human and animal. His concern for kittens and puppies, babies and lost humans of all ages began early and has not lost its strong pull toward saving the neglected or the troubled.

Along the way he met and became life-long friends with many persons of all genders, all ethnicities, the untethered, the weak and the strong, loved and unloved. Long ago that path connected with Steven Amedee who became a friend but he and Cary were not ready for a serious relationship. Fortunately, following years of learning life's lessons, their paths intersected again. Steven is a wonderful person who understood, brought forth the best, who loved and is loved by Cary and all the family. We were thankful and exceedingly grateful for the happy wonderment of this relationship, may it grow, strengthen and last through eternity.

In writing this history it was difficult for me to face my lifetime of memories where the wrong statement was uttered, the wrong advice proffered (unwanted, unheeded) and numerous poor outcomes resulted. If today's parents believed, by the time young adults headed to college, they were off the hook, so to speak, they would soon be disabused of that notion. It's more like you have reversed roles as years evaporate. My children began to give me advice about climbing ladders, mowing grass, driving in heavy traffic and myriad pursuits I have enjoyed for most of my ninety-two years. I, just like they, ignored sound advice and continued to do as I pleased.

I needed ten more years to enjoy my life, my loved ones, and make up for things done wrong, and right, replace the busy work of cooking and cleaning with the joy of taking more time for friends and relatives, too often neglected. There are many places I wanted to visit while I could still drive, walk, see, and hear. I enjoyed the great fortune of good health for decades but I can't count on that gift forever. If one person gained insight or benefitted in some way from reading this little history of a life, it was worth the writing. Thank you for following this account of a long life filled with despair and happiness, love and rejection, mountain tops and low swamps, weakness and power...and, above all, Love.

Chapter Ten

Back to Berry

Mount Airy, too boring for Al, and my reluctance to return to Buckhead, led the search for a town an easy drive from Atlanta, with active civic and social groups. Rome met, even exceeded, our requirements with sports and arts departments in three colleges. From Mount Airy we moved to Rome in 2002.

Fate brought me back where college life began fifty-six years earlier. I long expected to at least earn a BA degree and that goaded me to visit Berry's admissions office in 2005. I said I hoped credits earned in 1949-1950 might count and the astonished young man said, "We don't have records that old." He was thinking of computer records but I knew my information existed; all the credits were found and allowed. It was no easy slide going forward: astronomy, geology, foreign language, plus numerous literature and writing courses were required for graduation.

Two years later, addressing the audience as Valedictorian of the Class of 2007, I said, "If some of you parents have students on the five- or six-year plan, please don't give them a hard time. My Mother, who is here today, waited fifty-six years for me to graduate."

As an English major, I relished discussing the works of great authors. I had no plan to get a job or pursue a career. I had not considered the seduction of being offered a paid job upon graduation but I agreed to become executive director of the AIDS Resource Council. After two months on the job and looking at the financial records, I told the Board there was not enough money to pay me and provide the services needed but I would continue as the unpaid director as long as I could. Al was in his mid-nineties and I in my mid-seventies but I remained until Al's needs became foremost.

Before my final decision to enroll in Berry, Carol and I checked out assisted living facilities in Rome and Buckhead since we didn't want Al home alone while I attended class. We decided on a lovely new building in Buckhead on East Roxboro Road where social hour included wine, lunch out once a week for those who could manage, and it was on the route near Carol's home, where she ran almost daily. Al seemed happy there, participated in the activities until the day he decided to escape. From an upstairs window a resident saw Al crossing the front garden and putting out his thumb to get a ride. Fortunately, the driver realized what was happening (Al told him he didn't have his wallet and wanted to be dropped off at his bank to get money). The driver waited as staff dashed across the lawn to get Al who surreptitiously slipped out the door as visitors were leaving.

We decided it was safer to bring Al to Winthrop West in Rome, near Berry, where I sometimes joined him for lunch and brought him home on weekends. That routine worked for several months and soon after graduation I brought him home to stay for the remainder of his years. At his checkout I was given his things which included a shoebox full of pills, many unfamiliar. Back home that evening he became aggressive, threatening me, and I decided to sleep in the guest room. Some hours later he banged on my locked door, demanded to get in. I slipped out with the key in hand and locked him in. He finally fell asleep until he needed to go to the bathroom; I opened the door and as he came out, I went in and locked myself in the guest room. At last, he fell asleep in our old bedroom and slept for many hours, waking in an almost normal state of mind. After a couple of days, he returned to his pleasant, thoughtful self. I learned it was dangerous to suddenly withdraw psychosis-inducing drugs which were given to calm him at the facility when he insisted that he must go home. I was told nothing about drugs ordered for him by the facility or side effects of sudden withdrawal. I should have been forewarned; luckily no one was injured in his psychotic outburst.

The AIDS Resource Council which I managed and our home were one block apart on either side of the iconic Rome Clocktower. A neighbor was engaged to keep an eye on Al while I worked at ARC and I came home for lunch. Al enjoyed the Senior Center Wednesday lunch parties with live music, dancing, covered dish food, and bingo. When I had a work conflict and could not attend, I dropped him off and arranged for Rome's public curb-to-curb transportation service to pick up Al at the Center and drop him off at our house around 2 p.m. I went home from the office at that hour and the plan worked well until it didn't.

One afternoon I arrived home at 2 p.m. and there was no Al. I spoke to the neighbor; she had not seen the bus that often dropped him off. A call to the transportation department revealed the driver did pick him up at the Senior Center. Al insisted to the driver he was supposed to get off at the Georgia Power building, one of the busiest intersections in Rome. The driver was hesitant but Al convinced him that is where his wife was going to meet him. His guardian angel was on duty in the form of a neighbor passing by who saw Al walking downtown and took him home but Al did not stay at home. I phoned the police to look for a man of his description, and I began asking residents near our home if they had seen him.

At the third house—people we knew slightly—the man who answered my knock, asked with a smile, "Would you be referring to the white-haired gentleman asleep on my couch?"

That was Al's least frightening escapade away from his sitters and home but certainly not his last.

The next fright was arriving home a few weeks later finding Al and the Lincoln Town Car missing ...with both sets of car keys in my possession. Kirk, our grandson, phoned around 4 p.m. from the Bouley house in Buckhead and reported Al had come to Atlanta for a visit and he asked Kirk to let me know he was on his way back to Rome. I thought with Atlanta traffic he should be home by seven but instead I got a six-thirty message from William saying his dad called, reported he had stopped in Kennesaw at a Texaco station north of Atlanta to wait out a rain that made it hard to see. William offered to drive to Kennesaw to pick him up.

Al said, "No. I'm getting ready to leave now, the rain has stopped."

Worry increased; I adjusted my timeline to a nine-thirty arrival in Rome; at ten I called the police to report a person with dementia, missing and driving a car. An officer came to get particulars. He said they wait twenty-four hours before searching for someone missing but he would ask the Georgia Patrol officers along Highway 411 to watch for a green Lincoln Town Car.

I was afraid something terrible must have delayed Al. At eleven-thirty the Rome officer called to say my husband was fine and asked if someone could come to drive the car. I said I could call someone to help but he answered, "Don't worry, I'll park his car at the Ford dealership with a note it will be picked up in the morning. I will bring him home."

The officer performed an amazing act of kindness. When his shift ended, he didn't go home; he decided to drive to Highway 411 and watch for Al. He hadn't been there long when he saw a green Lincoln Town Car approaching from a side street and turning left into oncoming traffic. Realizing his mistake, Al pulled into the median where the officer stopped him. When I asked Al why he turned off 411 he said a stranger at the station in Kennesaw needed a ride to his house in Rome.

Al told him, "Get in, I'll take you home." Al's guardian angel was still on duty.

Al liked volunteering for Berry alumni work days. After he became unable to do many of the jobs, he enjoyed chatting with the other volunteers. We arrived at Oakhill—Martha Berry's home located on campus—to work on the upper garden but I didn't see anyone there. From his days in the South Pacific during WWII, Al's feet were always painful.

To save steps for him I said, "Wait here; I will check the sunken garden area."

In less than two minutes I returned to drive Al closer to the sunken garden only to discover Al and my car were not in sight, my handbag and phone left on the driver's seat. I asked a nearby Berry staff member if he saw Al leave.

"Yes. He said he was going to get his own car."

After finding someone with a phone, a call to the used car lot revealed Al was so insistent about needing to get to Berry, the office manager reluctantly gave him his key. My car was in their driveway with the door open; luckily my phone and purse were still on the seat. A friend drove me to my car. I phoned Berry security to keep him at the gate when he showed up. The Security guard laughed and asked if his car might have "Luxury Car for Sale" written across the windshield because that green Lincoln had already entered.

"If he tries to leave, don't open the gate; I'm on my way."

I told the dealership to sell that car no matter how cheap they had to go.

That episode couldn't compare with what came next. Our screened back porch was being converted to a sunroom by workmen we knew who understood Al's determination to drive. Again, I hired the neighbor to make the meals and keep an eye on Al so I could take a four-day trip to Provincetown, Cape Cod to visit Cary. Our locked van contained building materials for the porch and I gave a key to the workers. The morning before my scheduled return, I got a call from a worker saying the van and Al had disappeared, the key still in the worker's possession. I said notify the police; I will try to change my flight to come home today. Carol was calling hospitals and friends but no trace could be found. About 4:30 p.m. the neighbor phoned to tell me she saw a sheriff's car arrive and a deputy assisted Al up the front steps. I returned the next day and heard a tale that was both frightening and hilarious since Al was fine and no damage was done.

This is his account. He awoke early and wanted to see what was happening at the Senior Center but when he arrived no one was there so he decided to go to a center on Riverside Drive but he got lost. He was in a neighborhood where a woman in her bathrobe was getting her newspaper from the mailbox and he asked if she could direct him to the Senior Center. She replied no, but her husband was a policeman and she would call him for information. She probably thought Al was a weirdo, pulling up to her mailbox early in the morning in a dark van.

Al said he waited a long time; a policeman showed up and said, "I can't get you to that place but I can take you to visit the jail." Al replied that would be nice because the sheriff was a friend. He was put in the police car and our car was impounded. Al was taken to the county jail where he was photographed, fingerprinted, and put in a cell. He was asked to return to the intake area for another photograph and instructed not to smile this time. Asked if he wanted lunch, he said no.

Since he was just visiting, he would not be there very long. He told me it was a great visit to see how they do things since the days he was a sheriff in Florida. I was concerned about dehydration and asked if he was given any water. He said no, but the nice man in the room (he never realized it was a cell) showed him a button above the toilet where you could get drinking water.

Around 4 p.m. the sheriff arrived and a deputy told him, "You want believe this but there is a white-haired man here who claims he used to be sheriff of Duval County, Florida."

Sheriff Tim Burkhalter said, "Oh my God, get Al Cahill out of that cell and take him home."

Al never believed he was arrested, just given a thorough visit that demonstrated how things were done. We have the mugshot that says otherwise. I expressed serious concern to the court about the treatment of an elderly, confused person, who was locked up instead of taken to a hospital with no effort made to locate family. We were fortunate no harm was done; Al considered it a fine visit.

This episode did not deter Al's determination to drive but the mystery of car keys was solved when I picked up a nearly empty tissue box and found it to be heavy. With the remaining tissues removed, the bottom of the box contained numerous car keys.

I said to Al, "Look what I found."

He replied, "Hell, I didn't think you would ever look there."

He had numerous keys to each of our three vehicles in the box. Each time we took keys from him, he simply retrieved another set.

Al's ability to walk became increasingly problematic; he accepted a walking stick, resisted a walker. He was accustomed to going about in the neighborhood, to his barbershop, and visiting clergy at St. Peter's Episcopal Church all within a block of home. He enjoyed getting outdoors but all three entrances to our house had steps. One day, at the small porch of our Fifth Avenue entrance, I released his hand and placed it on the brick column for support while I unlocked the house door. I turned to take his hand but watched in horror as he fell backward to the concrete walk five feet below and landed on his head. I called 911, a nearby worker rushed across the street to help. Blood poured onto the walk; in less than four minutes, an ambulance arrived. At Floyd Hospital emergency it was determined there was no concussion, the wound was cleaned and bandaged; no stitches needed. After a few hours of observation, a nurse helped him sit up and dangle his feet.

After a few minutes she asked, "Can you walk?"

He replied "Yes."

She helped him stand. He put his arm around her waist, took her hand, and twirled her around. He thought she had asked, "Can you waltz?"

Staff couldn't suppress their laughter as the nurse replied, "If you can waltz, I guess you can walk."

He was discharged with no further treatment needed. A friend hearing this story remarked, "That's further proof you can't kill a Cahill."

It was apparent, with steps at every entrance in our home, Al would be isolated. I called Cary who was renovating a historic, hundred-year-old house in a transitional area of South Rome, located less than a mile away across the Etowah River. Cary replied the house was not ready, didn't have a kitchen. I said it had what was critical: a rear entrance with a half inch rise and no steps. We moved into the South Rome two-story house with four porches, wide hallways, and thirty-six-inch interior doors—wide enough for a wheelchair when one became necessary. For several years Al enjoyed the freedom of movement the house afforded him.

November 10, 2014, as Kirk and I held his hands, assuring him of our love and the time had come to let go. He puckered his lips for a kiss and took his last breath.

Our retired physician neighbor put the death in perspective when she said, "Jeanne do you realize how lucky you and Al were that he died with no pain, no illness but Alzheimer's?" He was 101 years old and never had a serious illness. Dr. Lucchese's words were comforting, and even more so now observing people in pain, dying, isolated from loved ones due to COVID-19.

My heart broke for the sufferer reaching and calling for family, and for loved ones who wanted to give comfort but must look on from a distance, unable to touch, or hold a hand. The death toll in the U.S. was over half a million mothers, fathers, sons, daughters, friends, relatives and strangers. A new way of life became necessary; isolation was mandatory as the ill could only look pleadingly toward loved ones behind glass or other barriers. Did the lonely, suffering patient understand why those they loved did not come to them? The patients were not alone in their grief and longing. Loved ones, family and friends of the ill were desolate, bereft of means to convey the love they felt and their desire to give comfort, especially to those who did not survive. The living carried a sad burden; they were prevented from holding, reassuring and wishing God's speed to those they loved as the last breaths were taken. The memories our grandparents told of the 1918 flu epidemic were replaced by the COVID-19 pandemic of 2020.

Fortunately, my family and I received the vaccines, wore masks, avoided crowds and escaped serious problems connected to the disease. A grateful "thank you" goes to the legions of professionals who cared for our loved ones, and who taught us how to survive.

Chapter Eleven

About Al

W illiam Alpheus "Al" Cahill was a complex man whose childhood was swept away by family circumstances and the Great Depression. His father, Alpheus, grew up on a Martinsville, Virginia plantation, went to work for the railroad in Roanoke where he met and married Hazel Lenore Jones, daughter of the railroad foreman. Henry Flagler brought Alpheus to the Florida Keys to help with the building of the Overseas Railroad. With only one highway out to higher land—the Cahill's lived on Marathon Key—women and children were moved to Miami for safety during hurricane season. On July 14, 1913, during Florida's hurricane season, baby "Al" was born at Biscayne Bay, Miami.

The family moved to New Smyrna Beach as the railroad was completed and father Alpheus became an engineer on a freight train carrying citrus fruit to New York. Speed predominated before refrigerated train cars were developed and perishables were afforded right-of-way. Florida's Bunnell Bypass allowed slower trains to pull off the main line for a fast train to pass on the single track. A train with mechanical problems, unable to notify the freight train it was disabled on the main track, sent a watchman down track with a lantern to signal the problem ahead. The watchman didn't go as far as instructed. He sat down, fell asleep, only awakened by sounds from the approaching train. He ran toward the speeding train, frantically swinging his warning lantern. Alpheus applied the emergency brakes, slid toward the unmoving train ahead, jumped before impact and landed on the watchman who did not survive. Alpheus was badly injured, narrowly escaping death.

He spent the next years in and out of hospitals, eventually moved to Jacksonville for treatment where he died in 1932, three years before Roosevelt signed Social Security into law. Widowed Hazel Lenore Jones Cahill, who had never had a job, struggled to raise three young children with no income, no social security or workmen's compensation. She wrote a column for the Daytona newspaper and young Al got a job daily sweeping out a grocery store in exchange for unsold produce. In time he added a paper route, sold magazine subscriptions and, as he became a teenager, worked at a drug store soda fountain.

He had a bike for delivering the newspapers and the local sheriff pressed him into service to obtain information about smugglers. The officers felt a kid on a bike could ride along the dirt road skirting the coastal inlets and report on boats with illegal contraband without alerting the smugglers. I don't know what the sheriff was looking for but the time was during prohibition, 1920 through 1933. The Florida coast—especially near small towns—was frequently a landing site for rum and other alcohol concoctions. More than once, Al was pressed into service and he reported the presence of boats.

For years he was the main support for his mother and two siblings until Ned Smullen, a Philadelphia salesman supplying products to funeral homes, met, fell in love with, and married Hazel. He moved to Jacksonville; a welcome addition to the Cahill family with children Al, Jefferson J., and Anna Lenore.

'Uncle Ned' met Al and Hazel through the Cooper Funeral Home where Al worked to pay his father's 1932 funeral expenses. Upon high school graduation Al was offered a scholarship to Georgia School of Technology but his meager income was critical to his family. Prior to Ned's arrival, college was not an option. The youngest Florida licensed embalmer, (he waited for his twenty-first birthday to receive his license) Al became director of the funeral home. Well known and well liked throughout Jacksonville, he volunteered at the Episcopal Church, was on a swim team, and a Scout Master.

Popular with the debutante society in Jacksonville, Al was invited to the best parties. He attributed his popularity to having a fine car and a black suit—thanks to being a funeral director. I am sure he was invited because he was handsome, a gentleman in every way, and a good dancer.

A fine car and nice suit didn't hurt.

These happy times for him were short lived as problems in Europe grew ominously and the likelihood of U.S. involvement in the war in Europe became imminent. When Pearl Harbor was bombed, Al knew he would be in the first draft—young, healthy, no dependents, embalming skills needed in war, so he enlisted in the Navy.

Frances McIntire Hollahan, a young widow with a son, had other ideas. She met Al when he conducted the funeral of her young husband who died of a heart attack. She called frequently to invite Al to her home, to advise, to help her make decisions about raising her son, and she didn't want Al to enlist. Al said she worked on his sympathy and talked him into marriage although he preferred to wait until after the war. Al spent the dangerous war years in the South Pacific assigned to a Marine unit as a Navy medic, the favorite target of Japanese in the palm trees as troops waded ashore. Shooting medical team members turned out to be a successful tactic used by the Japanese to demoralize the troops.

At the war's end, he received a 100 percent medical disability discharge, followed by almost a year of therapy at Glenwood Springs, Colorado. Daily he swam to exhaustion in the hot spring-fed Olympic-sized pool. He was determined to get home, find a new career, and get to know the woman he married three years earlier. Al returned to Jacksonville and was hired by an insurance agency where he could work seated. Due to his painful feet, he could no longer perform the heavy lifting required of a funeral director/embalmer. He soon became the top producer in the insurance company.

Although they had been separated for nearly three years, Frances chose to not visit Al in Colorado. Al said he returned to a stranger who was his wife. In my presence she sometimes bragged about having fun with the officers at the Jacksonville USO during the years Al faced constant danger from Japanese sharpshooters. She wrote only two letters to Al during those long months he was in the South Pacific; she said she didn't write because she objected to censors reading her V-mail.

Al was highly successful in the insurance industry, soon established his own agency and became a leader in the corporate business arena. In addition to serving on several civic boards, he was elected president of the Jacksonville Jaycees, then Florida Jaycees, and was named One of Ten Outstanding Young Men of Florida. As a board member of Jaycees International, Al took a group of young leaders from the U.S. on a globe circling trip to encourage young men in war-torn countries to organize and become the leaders in rebuilding their homelands. In spite of painful feet, his unbounded energy always kept him striving for a better world.

Another of his notable achievements brought the Freedom Train to Jacksonville in 1947, displaying this country's most important documents. Cities to be visited were required to agree to no segregated viewing in any form; failing such assurance a city would be bypassed. Memphis's refusal to integrate viewing eliminated the train's visit to Tennessee. Al's leadership was instrumental in the documents arriving in Jacksonville where school buses brought hundreds of students to see the original Bill of Rights, the Constitution, and the Emancipation Proclamation.

He convinced the city fathers to accept the requirement for no segregated viewing during the time the documents were in Jacksonville. Al told me he was a greeter at the entrance to make sure every guest was treated to the same warm welcome. As one of the visiting students, he must have spoken to me, twenty-two years before we were married. I remember the documents; I don't remember the greeter.

His strong-held belief segregation was wrong was again demonstrated when, in 1957 as sheriff, he hired the first black detectives to serve in that capacity before there was a mandate to integrate. Al never forgot the hardships his family endured and he was empathetic toward anyone struggling to succeed on an uneven playing field. He occupied the role of breadwinner before he was a teenager. Perhaps his Great Depression experiences of responsibility, work, and following orders created too much emphasis on teamwork to the detriment of freedom and creativity our children wanted and needed.

What I knew was his unending pride and love of our children while failing to see their need for independence and for choices of their making. I was not confident enough of my ideas to take a strong stand sooner on William's behalf in his formative years. For Carol and Cary, Al was much more understanding, demanded less regimentation and I interceded more often.

William became hardened and closed off from family activities at an early age. Recently he told me he was never listened to as a teenager and even younger. Apparently, he believed his only control was to refuse to participate, not join family activities.

He recently told me a Christmas story that hurt my heart. He wanted a new bike, the old one worn and too small. He was a middle schooler, rode around our neighborhood with friends. We bought a pretty good one, similar but larger than his old bike. He didn't want to hurt our feelings but he was secretly devastated because it didn't have gears. He said he had to struggle to keep up with his friends as they sailed up and down hills and he had to work harder on a bike built for level, undemanding areas. He felt his friends had grownup bikes and his was for a kid on a sidewalk. That was over fifty years ago and the scar is still in him. I wanted to cry; we were well-meaning but we should have listened more carefully or sought information and prevented half a century of sad remembrance for him.

Al was an outstanding father of our children when they were very young. Playful and energetic, he crawled around with little ones on his back, swam with them hanging on, taught them to dive while they were malleable and followed his directions. When Lynda lived with us, he had four acolytes—Paula, Carol, Karen, and Cary, ages five to three. William was often the loner, with a four-year gap in age between him and the next child. Once again, I failed to acknowledge how this apparently added to his feeling of spectator more than participant.

Al's expectations were often not met as the children grew and began to think for themselves, to make their own decisions. Adolescence arrived with a tug of war between what the children wanted and what their father expected. I accepted blame for not taking a stronger stand sooner on their behalf; I often walked a narrow line trying to keep the peace. On balance Al deserved praise for love and generosity. He earned high marks for innumerable acts of kindness and being true to what he earnestly thought was right for family, friends, and strangers.

We did not understand there was a better way than the old one by which we were raised.

In chapters five and six I wrote about meeting and falling in love with Al while he was the sheriff of Duval County. He was the ultimate gentleman—thoughtful, caring, and generous—if you were not breaking a law. His friends, neighbors, and relatives quickly learned they got no preferential treatment; the law was the same for everyone. He never wavered and the requests for special favors stopped coming.

My reluctance to intercede earlier on behalf of our first child probably resulted somewhat from Al being my boss three years earlier, plus at twenty years my senior I acquiesced to his experience. Perhaps that bore some truth ... or it was my excuse? At any rate, Al was accustomed to giving orders and expecting them to be obeyed.

One reason he wanted to live in a big house was to have lots of company and frequent parties: some just for fun, many for charity fund-raising, others to raise funds for progressive politicians. When we bought our first home, Al purchased a long, red-carpet runner which he rolled out for every party. He told me Frances never allowed parties or receptions in their home; she would call one of their private clubs and turn over all details to a third party. He was surprised—and pleased—to learn the Taylor clan seemed to always have relatives or friends visiting. He was relieved to discover I rarely said "no" to any opportunity to invite friends or strangers to our home.

In the mid-sixties, Lenox Square was a prominent open-air mall less than a mile from our home and the children loved to climb on the large concrete figures from the Uncle Remus story. There was always outdoor entertainment around holidays and Al introduced the children to the performers and invited the out-of-towners to our home for Thanksgiving or Christmas. A four-member family of ice skaters, a ventriloquist, a singer, and our Secretary of State, Max Cleland, to name a few who were with us at Christmas times, all personally invited by Al.

Our most interesting and most unanticipated group consisted of twelve Russian Olympic gold medalists visiting the U.S. promoting the 1984 Games. We were invited to a dinner dance for them in an Atlanta hotel and through interpreters I learned this was the last event in their travels from California to Atlanta then Moscow. They had only been in hotels; not entertained in a private home and I inquired of the State Department if it would be permissible for the Russian leader to select twelve to come to our home the following evening for a buffet supper. "Yes" was the answer, our work was cut out for us and Al was thrilled. The next morning, we invited twelve neighbors to participate: some to follow Al to the hotel to pick up the guests; help for me with cooking, flower arranging, table setting, etc. By 7 p.m. our house we called "the shed" was abuzz with activity as the incredulous guests observed its comfort, accommodations, and the indoor swimming pool.

Their leader who spoke English said rather haughtily to me, "Of course, we understand most Americans don't live like this."

I replied: "You are right. Many Americans live much better. We are considered middle-class."

She did not make any more comments about our living conditions. The guests were grateful, appreciative of our efforts. Little did we know the Soviet invasion of Afghanistan would lead President Carter to bravely, reluctantly, boycott the Games.

He was joined by sixty-five nations that refused to participate in the Games. I still have the Olympic pins given to us featuring Misha, a lovable cuddly bear Soviets hoped would counter the Russian bear image of strength and superiority. Al was in his element, red carpet out, shuttling guests, and through interpreters, discussing the sports in which our guests excelled and received gold medals.

This was not the only time I was responsible for giving him a last-minute mountain of responsibilities. The next time was a fund-raising party in the late 1970s for the Marietta Symphony Guild. I never worried about turning a project over to him. If he agreed, you could count on it being done well. His un-flagging energy and resourcefulness in meeting any challenge resulted in success.

Four days before the Guild party a call came from the Friendship Force stating two FF Ambassadors had a problem and could not go to Costa Rica for two weeks. An urgent call from Rosalynn Carter's office indicated Rosalynn and her mother, Mrs. Smith, were leading the exchange and asked if I could help. Host families expected the two Ambassadors and organizers were desperate for replacements and hoped I could fill in. I said "Yes" and called my neighbor, Sonja Lazzaro who was as spontaneous as I and we set out on a perk-filled adventure.

Participants could choose to stay one week with each of two families or have one week on your own. We chose the latter and went to a hotel in San Jose for the second week. At check-in we were behind a twenty-year-old golfer with Atlanta tags on his golf bag. He heard our Georgia voices and introduced himself, Tim Simpson, said he was part of the PGA tour located at the Cariari Country Club just outside the city and would be pleased to designate us as his guests with club house passes and transportation from the hotel. Riding to the club with hotel workers, we were soon identified by them as Rosalynn Carter and Julie Andrews and asked for autographs. Sonja wrote Rosalynn but I wrote my own name.

The club was beautiful and surrounded by luxurious homes. Tim said golfers and their guests were invited for dinner at several of the homes and we accompanied him to one lovely party. We were invited to ride back to our hotel with Jesus Rodriguez, brother of Chi Chi. It was a special day and evening but we declined the invitation to accompany Jesus R. to any additional festivities. The next evening was even more interesting with a symphony performance across the park from our hotel. Sonja knew a member of the symphony who previously played with Atlanta Symphony Orchestra. At the box office we were not allowed to pay for tickets but were escorted up a beautiful staircase to a private box near the center of the horse shoe as the only patrons there. Our curiosity was soon answered when the President's party was seated in the adjoining box. I think it was in Luis Guillermo Solis's term in office. A spotlight was put on the President; he stood and bowed, then the spotlight was on us. Sonja and I stood and bowed and we were applauded as the president had been. We had no idea what the Spanish message was.

At intermission we went downstairs to inquire about Sonja's friend from ASO and were escorted to a dressing room where the friend soon appeared. Sorry I don't remember his name but he sent a car the following evening to take us to his home on a mountainside overlooking San Jose. We had a lovely dinner cooked by his housekeeper over an outdoor open fire. The view was spectacular. Soon we rejoined the Friendship Force ambassadors for the return to Atlanta.

Back at home, Al, with help from Guild members, managed the party for fifty-plus guests. The party was a huge success and the Guild members expressed great admiration for Al's handling of everything. He loved a reason to roll out his red carpet.

Al had legions of friends but he didn't hesitate to be bluntly truthful to anyone he felt needed to be called out. He occasionally said, "I'm not here to win a popularity contest. If someone acts like a fool, I feel a duty to tell him he's a fool." He was filled with knowledge because he would ask for information about anything from anybody. He was only 5 feet 7 inches tall but he was a larger-than-life amazing human being. I can't recall any request from me being met with a "no." The freedom we gave each other added to the success of our fifty-five-year marriage.

About Wannie deserved more than this brief notation; she appeared throughout my story in uncounted ways. She was the central influence in our lives—love of music and dancing, curiosity about everything, aspirational thinking. She could have been a gymnast; in her fifties she could still turn a perfect cartwheel and, in her sixties, she asked for a bike as her birthday gift. She wanted to try hitting a golf ball on the farm's three-hole golf course Al made for the children to learn the basics of playing golf. He showed her how to hold the club and swing at the ball. On her first attempt the ball landed in the cup and she asked, "Is that what I was supposed to do?"

She broke her leg as a teenager learning to ride a bike but her greatest mistake occurred with her daddy's loaded shotgun which always stood behind the front door. When she was thirteen, she saw a bush filled with birds at the edge of the yard and decided to shoot. She knew a gun had a kick back so she held it away from her as far as she could reach and pulled the trigger. Her four front teeth were knocked out and it took weeks for false teeth to be made but Grandmother Mary Jane made her go to school, humiliated by missing teeth.

She was always teaching us as we went about our daily chores. When toilet paper was purchased for the outhouse at the service station, she had Gloria and me observe her rolling off three little squares, folding each end over the center. She said to do that and clean front to back, never back to front. I rarely enter a bathroom without remembering her lesson. She was most adamant about speaking clearly and correctly; no slang was allowed. Gloria once told mother I was cursing in front of some playmates. I was chastised for saying heck. I miss her still. All these years later I continue to conduct myself according to her teaching, her composure in the face of life's vicissitudes.

Chapter Twelve

#7 Lookout Avenue, South Rome

Al preferred large houses regularly filled with relatives and other guests. In spite of its incomplete status when we moved in, Al was happy with the size and accommodations of #7 Lookout Avenue, built in 1910. The downtown 'clocktower' house in which we lived was a normal three-bedroom bungalow about which he frequently said, "This place isn't big enough."

The day he lost his balance and landed upside down on the concrete sidewalk I, too, agreed the house with three entrances, steps at each, was no longer acceptable. After five happy years it was time for a change. Al was quite pleased with the prospect of six bedrooms, two parlors, and all the usual accommodations of a large house, beautifully restored by Cary.

A progressive community welcomed us to our new neighborhood where we felt at home from the beginning, and where Al could walk out the back door with only a walking stick for balance. The Between the Rivers/Clocktower neighborhood we left was close enough to stay in contact with friends there and #7 Lookout Avenue provided a new activist group of friends. My mother instilled in me the riches of having many friends, especially those younger who had a better chance of being around into my advanced years. Great advice! I have scores of young friends that keep me younger than I have a right to be. Thank Heaven!

A strong disagreement existed between residents and South Rome Redevelopment Agency/Corporation (SRRC) regarding development along the Etowah River. Residents wanted to follow the recommendation to turn the area into an arts colony as designed by Georgia Tech land planners in a study commissioned by the city. SRRC wanted instead to demolish the modest workers' homes to make way for an affordable housing senior high-rise building.

As experienced activists, we joined the fray and soon admired our civic-minded, tenacious neighbors. A long battle ensued but, in the end, the opposition won. Our community could no longer afford expensive legal fees, and had no choice but to accept a compromise with only one house saved and the high-rise built. The playing field was not fair; we paid a lawyer, and our taxes paid the city's opposing lawyer. We lost the battle but enduring bonds of friendship developed. Several of us continued to attend SRRC board meetings and I was surprised when invited to become a member of the board. I served three terms; the maximum one can serve continuously. We were not opposed to affordable housing for seniors. There were many available sites for the new housing without eliminating modest houses of the workers who basically built the downtown area. You can't win all the civic battles but it was hard to give up the dream of an arts community along the banks of the Etowah.

Several months after moving to South Rome, it became apparent Al needed 24-hour observation and the entire family wanted the best possible quality of life for him. Kirk Bouley, our grandson who had a heart as big as Al's, called from Asia to say he would soon come home. He traveled abroad for eighteen months after graduating Mercer University; a trip paid for with money accumulated by selling all his possessions. While he was in Asia, he wanted to visit Thailand but money was running low with only enough remaining for airfare home. He offered to live with me and help with Al in exchange for travel costs to visit Thailand. I immediately said yes. For the next couple of years, he was a huge help and Al and I were grateful for his presence.

As Al took his last, easy breaths, Kirk and I were holding his hands and assuring him it was okay to release himself from the struggle to breathe. November 10, 2014, Al was 101 years old. We were married more than half a century, leaving a void that can't be filled but that doesn't mean I am sad. It would have been selfish to ask for more of the time he generously gave to many, especially to me, in his long and productive life.

Kirk's help was a gift to me and a selfless gesture to Al in his final months. He was great help and a joy to have with us during a period of absorbing the experiences of his extensive travels and looking ahead with the big question of what is next. If Al were here, he would join me in expressing appreciation for Kirk's help and love to the last moment.

With Al's demise I committed to working more earnestly on this memoir but it has been sporadic. I often found myself weeding the garden, adding another flower, laying a brick walkway and believing if I can keep plants thriving, surely, I can help my loved ones thrive.

William's declining health was a stressful concern as he reluctantly gave up his interests, realizing his active, pain-free years were gone and the headache and fading strength were ever-present. He lived on a farm west of Rome where scrawny pines and lush weeds obscured former pastures, where old outbuildings groaned, leaned toward the ground until they gave up.

He struggled to breathe and used his diminishing energy to tolerate pain and maintain himself while leaving the smallest possible carbon footprint as a gift to future generations. I made bi-weekly visits, shopped for groceries, cooked things for the freezer, helped with small projects, and cleaned (but never enough to pass my inspection) and assisted with small projects. It was a lonely, isolated life which he spent creating tables and small table toppers from fragrant juniper salvaged from a fallen tree, and grew plants including rare chiltepin peppers and tomatoes. The round trip to the farm was eighteen miles from the South Rome house, an easy drive that left time for my other tasks.

Friday afternoon, March 13, 2020, no email in or out for two days raised a red flag. I bumbled through a few clicks hoping to find the problem when "Click here for help" appeared and the accompanying phone number led to someone answering "Google technical assistance" who asked about my problem. The time was mid-afternoon, Friday. I knew a little about scammers, phishing, other ways to trick vulnerable people, especially elderly women. I was not prepared for three clever men with plausible answers to every question. I will skip details of a two-hour exchange during which they convinced me I needed third-party software and it wouldn't be available until the following week if they didn't get the order in before 5 p.m.

When I said I didn't have $2,100 in my checking account they "got permission" to accept three payments of $700 each with two checks postdated. With trepidation I wrote one $700 check with some numbers following the name "Google," held it to the screen but refused the post-dated checks. The 'technicians' began 'restoring' my email account and my screen showed rapid downloading. I called a neighbor, Jon Hershey, and he called our expert friend, Chad Jonfroe, for help to stop the download. Within a few minutes, with Chad's telephoned direction, downloading stopped. I was relieved it was 4:10 p.m., the bank would be closed. Jon and Chad saved me from financial loss. Still awake at midnight, worried over how much info was downloaded, I went on line and transferred all but $10 from checking to a HELOC account. No money was lost and I learned a lesson. Jon and Chad, young friends, were my heroes.

Due to the rapid spread of COVID-19, quarantine was finally imposed after pressure was put on President Trump who declared a National Emergency on March 13, 2020, and asked for two weeks of self-quarantining. It was too little too late to prevent the mounting death toll. Instead of following CDC guidelines, Trump recommended dangerous "snake oil" cures and put economy ahead of saving lives. South Rome neighbors and I stayed in our houses. Jon Hershey and Paula Blalock were my angels of mercy throughout the quarantine for which I was most grateful.

A few years earlier when Trump became the presidential nominee of the Republican Party, there was considerable opposition in the neighborhood. For me it meant political signs of opponents in my yard, cards written, phone calls made. I hoped he could not possibly be elected due to his personal foibles and lack of qualifications. I had not counted on the plethora of racists, sexists, homophobes, other haters. There were some good people that refused to become informed, who became Trump's primary sycophants and acolytes, convinced he was their savior.

Legions of good Republicans sat on their hands and voted to keep their party in office. Thousands of historians, journalists, scientists of many disciplines, theologians, and others chronicled the damage wrought by Trump. I am unqualified to add more. Numerous historians called him the worst president this country has ever had.

With the quarantine lifted I considered the work entailed in keeping a big house with only me in it plus the labor to maintain a sizable yard. Carol continued her effort to have me live closer to her in Atlanta's Hapeville area. That coincided with a repeated request from friends that wanted to buy #7 Lookout Avenue. I acquiesced and moved to Atlanta's Hapeville area in July, 2021.

Like countless thousands of the elderly, primarily women living alone, I joined the migration to live with or at least near my daughter. I understood all the reasons such a move made sense but that made the decision no easier. It broke my heart to realize what must be disposed of and to see things I felt attached to going out the door with strangers. Will the person holding my beautiful maidenhair fern remember it needs water every day? I told him what I was told. "If you go on vacation, take the fern with you or it will be dead when you return."

The sorting, packing, and giving away seemed insurmountable but with generous help from neighbors and relatives, the exodus began in earnest. Friends Susan Carlson and Linda Williams spent untold hours packing all the fragile crystal, china, silver, and breakable art objects. Their care resulted in valuables arriving intact in boxes unpacked. Nearly two years have passed while the storage building behind my Hapeville house still contains unopened boxes.

Obviously, I should have disposed of more. Cary made trips from New York whenever possible to help with hundreds of details and to take the few pieces for which he had room. Carol also took what she could use while many items went on the porch and sidewalk with a "FREE" sign. The bigger the house, the bigger the mountain of stuff. I concluded one needs a two-year period to sort through and dispose of the flotsam and jetsam of big house living ... and begin the downsizing as early as possible. If I had followed any part of such knowledge, I would have had fewer feelings of loss.

A life-enriching experience lifted my spirits when I walked three short blocks from my new home to visit The Village Church and heard Ray Waters deliver a sermon. I thought, "How does he know what is burdening me?" What I realized was I found my new tribe and time has strengthened that belief. I had a roster of new, loving friends and my former neighbors and friends were a click or seventy miles away. It's a lesson in embracing the "new" while honoring the "familiar."

August, 2022, the pressure was on to complete this story, following two years of neglect. My short-term memory deficit became apparent, recent names more difficult to recall, recent events less sharp, elusive, and time was of the essence. Amazingly, happenings of eighty or more years ago were often in sharper focus than the name of the person I just met. I lived three blocks from my thoughtful and generous daughter and I had an increasing number of lovely new friends but it wasn't the same as friends with whom I shared history. I don't regret the move even as I grieve a bit. The therapy of gardening came along but so did concern for our Democracy.

Chapter Thirteen

Triple Whammy

T rump, along with the Pillow Man and others, trumpeted ridiculous cures for COVID-19. I noticed an oddity in Trump's statements; he didn't say "do this or take that" but rather made it sound like something one should consider, thereby laying the groundwork for denial when his 'cures' were shown to be worthless and often dangerous. Soon much of the population went into self-imposed quarantine with California the first state to issue a stay-at-home order, March 19, 2020. President Trump said it was like a cold, or mild flu, and would disappear by April. Companies put fattening their bottom line ahead of saving lives. As I wrote this, 1,123,613 Americans died because of COVID-19. It did not, and will not, disappear completely as Trump claimed.

Humanitarianism disappeared from the White House. The recommended mask wearing was eschewed by many, especially the president, as the virus continued unabated. In my opinion Trump has blood on his hands by ignoring the seriousness of the pandemic and by abetting violence through lies about the 2020 election.

He brazenly proclaimed, without anything to back it up, he won the election by a landslide. Throughout the country, judges at all levels, governors and attorneys general of both parties repeatedly labeled these wild statements as untrue but

Trump repeated the lies until his followers believed him. These lies apparently led to insurrection on January 6, 2021.

Voltaire's prescient words say it best: "Anyone who can make you believe absurdities can make you commit atrocities."

From Garry Kasparov: "When a leader lies constantly, the goal isn't to make you believe something, it's to make you believe anything."

The insurrectionist attack on the Capitol has been covered millions of times in books, columns, articles, and social media. Encouraged by the president and his minions, the criminal perpetrators called patriots, downplayed the mayhem and deaths. The illegal, shocking, and disgraceful law-flaunting attack on our Constitution and the Capitol was a frightening view of the underbelly of hatred and political ignorance across the country.

Georgia surprised the nation by electing two Democratic senators and President Joseph Biden, turning the state blue and changing the hierarchy in Washington. I was jubilant over the outcome of the election but saddened about friends and relatives supporting a liar, criminal, disgraced egotist, twice impeached charlatan, protected from expulsion by Republicans that apparently feared loss of position and money if they crossed him. Politics before "we the people" is not sustainable.

President Biden inherited serious problems with COVID-19 deaths, the economy, the hungry and unemployed, a tax structure benefiting the rich while many in the middle class slid into poverty. I believed he was up to the task to lead this nation into a new level of leadership at home and regain prominence on the world stage. A primary obstacle in that path was the number of office holders frightened they will fall off the "gravy train" if they don't remain sycophants along with Trump's "kiss the ring" toadies.

Especially troubling were injustices visited upon the poor, especially the minority poor, and if we didn't find that path to better lives, we were in for difficult times. My fantasy was to hear a loud "I am terribly sorry" from every individual that aided and abetted DJT as he occupied the most powerful position on Earth. His sordid, ignoble acts were already on public record for all to see along with his ignorance of government, geography, and history for starters.

His strong suit was in theatrics and self-promotion, reminding me of a quote about the Pied Piper in the German fairy-tale: "Trailing after the hypnotic notes of the rat-catcher's magical flute, the rodents politely filed through the city gates to their presumed doom." Raphael Kadushin. The critical difference in that scenario is mayhem and murder in our Capitol on January 6, 2021, no polite filing out of town.

What has not changed is my dismay over much-loved relatives and friends who supported—and probably still do—the person many historians called "the worst president this country has ever had." He isn't just a little worse, he is a load of crap worse as a bumper sticker observed: "The country has run out of toilet paper because President Trump is full of s—t."

Native Americans gave us a beautiful reminder in the belief "We do not inherit the Earth from our ancestors; we borrow it from our youth."

Our environment and our government are fragile and must be carefully protected. Growing pains were bound to occur and surrendering old ways of being was not easy; it was necessary. I saw the determination in my house guests consisting of my granddaughter Ladybird, her partner and child. They were far better recyclers, reducers, reusers, and repurposers than I and most of my generation. This new youthful generation set the bar high; we of the old habits better learn to jump or get out of the way, surrender the playing field to younger leaders.

In my ninety-two years the changing landscape evolved from no electricity on the southern farms of my grandparents, to rockets cavorting around Mars. My great-grandson will someday make similar comparisons to the then and now of his world. He and his numberless cohorts must exploit—in a positive way—the abundance not only of the Earth, but of vast, unimaginable outer-limits of space. I hope my Spirit-self can observe the cataclysmic and miraculous evolution of a changed world living peacefully with all the disparate inhabitants.

My personal world space underwent a change during the writing of my story. Carol persuaded me that continuing alone in a large house and garden, and the work required to keep them up was not the best future for me. My buyers had a buyer for their home and they needed to vacate rapidly. Hasty winnowing began in earnest. Family members were invited to take things, Dogwood Books paid $100 for two boxes of fine books with regional connections, and a few others bought accessories and art objects. My earnings amounted to less than $500 for the impromptu unannounced 'sale.' Family members loaded up whatever they wanted. Signs for "FREE STUFF" were placed on South Broad Street and the front steps of my house.

The mountain of goods became a small hill. One sad challenge was placing the beautiful Chickering piano. No takers even free and delivered! My best offer was from a man with a truck. He offered to haul it to the landfill for $800. I was ready to call a woodworker friend to salvage the wood and carvings when the phone rang. A family from Alabama asked if the piano was still available. Two hours later it was on their truck and the house was empty except for items I agreed to leave. Hardest to part with was the dining room suite; not many homes can accommodate a seven-foot marble top buffet plus server, china cupboard, table and chairs. The new owners were happy to have those and numerous other items I agreed to leave behind.

I have not been inclined to have a dinner party since moving into my present house in August, 2022. Crystal, china, and silver stored in packing boxes wait in the building called "the barn" located behind the historic house I bought in tiny

Hapeville. Maps understandably show the world's largest airport—Hartsfield-Jackson— to be in Atlanta. The city grew beyond its boundaries, encompassing Hapeville and numerous small municipalities now sharing Atlanta zip codes. Many residents are proud of their town and have the choice of traditional name, or use Atlanta; hence my actual location is historic Hapeville. The day before Thanksgiving, over two and a half million passengers were scheduled to pass through the airport. All day long, from my east-facing windows, I watched a sky dotted with planes landing and departing. The only area in the terminal with no lines was International; proof that Thanksgiving is truly the holiday for visiting family and loved ones, eschewing exotic places abroad in favor of grandmother's cornbread or pumpkin pie. On an average day there are 2,700 arrivals and departures carrying 275,000 passengers. Amazingly, the noise factor at my house was minimal even on high air traffic days.

In moving from a spacious home I admired and enjoyed, I joined millions of women who made a similar decision late in life. I have no great wisdom to share but I learned the importance of flexibility and a willingness to speak up and change if needed. Downsizing sounds easy but don't kid yourself; it's not. There are experts all over the internet anxious to tell you how to handle the task for any attic, basement, garage, room, or closet. They don't tell you how to fast forward your grief at parting with a life's collection of memories. It hurts, it's difficult. Don't wait until the last minute to give a niece that bracelet she admired, or your cousin the vase she borrowed for parties. Start early to separate your sheep from your goats and take pleasure in making others happy instead of the coldness of $2 from a yard sale.

My kind, generous, and lovely daughter had for some time attempted to convince me to stop spending so much time living alone.

"Come live with me. You can sit by the pool, read, relax, leave everything to me, and enjoy life." She wisely added, "If that isn't to your liking we can find a house nearby for you."

I agreed before I learned my house must turn over so rapidly. I thought of friends who had an amazing "house-cooling party" when they were leaving the country for two years. Guests were prohibited from bringing anything; before they could leave, they must take something from pantry, bar, or bathrooms ... things not suited to storage. One more good idea I didn't have time to pull off. Sitting by the pool wasn't on my radar because I like to be busy but that was not the reason for rethinking my situation. I liked every food I encountered, exotic or commonplace—with the exception of a runny egg—but hadn't considered what living with a vegan and her list of allergies would mean. I soon realized we would remain good friends if we had separate kitchens.

Three blocks from my daughter's home stood an historic house for sale. Once again, I began the familiar work of making a very old house, late 1800s, into a home for myself. Sounds crazy, but I am happier digging crabgrass than sitting by her pool. That pool and garden area became the setting for a fabulous ninetieth birthday party Carol held for me in October attended by nearly 100 friends from both neighborhoods—Rome and Hapeville.

My new 'old' house, on the main street in the heart of Hapeville was selected as an investment; everything around me is commercial and it's a matter of time until I get the right offer. I had no set notion of the next location to follow these decades of an overloaded calendar but decision time can't be far away. If I am to visit, to travel as I indicated was my wish, I had to finish writing this family story for Lynda and Sandy. They were the first to ask for an account of the family journey before they were born thus the story you are reading. These are my memories (with validation from the welcome Internet), of eighty-four years from the depths of the Great Depression to concern over Artificial Intelligence plotting the future of Earth.

Chapter Fourteen

Moving On

Wisdom from a New Generation

Writing the stories of my family surprised me in unexpected ways, including my failure to see numerous errors of judgment as events occurred. My parents were loving and kind, doing what they thought best, following the footsteps of their parents born in the late 1800s.

Collectively they lived through World War One, the flu pandemic of 1918, came of age and married during the Great Depression, the time of my birth. From them I inherited a work ethic and the importance of living up to what was expected of us as children. There were no hard rules to be followed but we were to be obedient, to be pleasant, and follow our parents' instructions.

Lying was not an option ... it never occurred to me to try it. All of Dixie Union was within earshot of a strong adult voice; news of misbehavior traveled at warp speed.

I knew I was in trouble for once again scratching Gloria's arm when she dawdled over some chore we shared. I decided to run away rather than face Mother's disappointment over my impatience with Gloria. A five-year-old isn't a good planner but I knew it would soon become dark and I didn't want to be too far away at night. The tool shed behind Daddy's repair garage seemed far enough and I thought I could slip into the kitchen when I got hungry. Eventually, I heard my name loudly called by my parents; adult neighbors joined in and also began calling my name as they walked to all the houses. I knew I was caught when they came closer to my hiding place. I opened the door and stepped out to the worried countenances of Dixie Union's populace.

There was such relief, my parents forgot to punish me. They thought some tourists might have snatched me into their car. I tried to look contrite.

In our small hamlet there were no young children outside of the Taylor "bunch." As my "running away" demonstrated, residents were aware of any happening and joined in when help was needed. We were products of the generations before us, reflections of the upbringing of our parents and grandparents.

I desired to give my own children a life of ease, and more opportunities afforded by a degree of prosperity. None of this worked out as I imagined. I was in my late 80s when I first heard the words, "unschooling, and "intentional living and learning." Observing today's young parents, I saw where I went off the rails. I never allowed my children to make their own decisions; I did it for them. I anticipated their needs when they were toddlers and did what I believed best but I couldn't have been more misguided. If it was 11 a.m., "I must cook lunch," was my first thought without considering if anyone was actually hungry or wanted what I prepared. Our pediatrician didn't want commercial baby food given to his little patients. "It's getting cool. Put on a sweater," when I might have been the only one feeling cool. "Hold my hand so you won't trip," when there were steps, or stones in the path. During those early stages of development, I did not allow independence, self-reliance or learning the consequences of one's decisions or actions.

In retrospect, it's easy to see our three babies' lives were too regimented, too organized, with far too much hovering by the parents, especially by me. There was a schedule for waking up, mealtime, naps and bedtime. I can't change any of what went before; I can only say I am sorry for things I did or failed to do to allow our children to develop their own best selves earlier, in their own way. I am saddened and contrite over my ill-conceived "help" denying them the opportunity to "discover."

In another chapter I wrote about signing up the children for sports to help develop a sense of teamwork; basically, they disliked all the choices we made for them. None of the three cared about the team sports they endured; felt they must tolerate. Al and I had too much old school thinking. Today's parents are not as tied to tradition. There are more appropriate concerns in understanding the child's interests and facilitating that interest with creative activity of the child's choosing. I regret I denied my children important learning opportunities at the beginning of their lives. The past is indeed prolog with an abundance of knowledge to use in whatever number of days are mine to live. It can't be many with a ninetieth birthday already celebrated but I was recently given a gem of wisdom.

I opined to a friend how my life turned upside down these past few years as I gave up a beautiful historic home, moved away from familiarity, and now live in a house I don't like very much, an investment, but here I am. I thought I would die in a home—lovely and loved— filled with the keepsakes of a lifetime, surrounded by the people I deeply cared for. I am fortunate with many of the people still here but keepsakes are scattered, or sealed in packing boxes.

The friend's wise response: "If you had died ten years ago Jeanne, you would have had all that."

What a perfect rejoinder, the exact words I needed to hear as I recalled the joys, the experiences of the decade. For starters, I would not have known my five-year-old great-grandson who has brought immeasurable joy to me and to all of our clan. The tradeoff was greatly in my favor: my replacement house was acceptable; the keepsakes grew fainter in memory and importance as I focused forward with time for stories recalled but not yet written. I haven't found a discernible stopping point as I continued being and doing the things I enjoyed. Most mornings if the calendar was blank, I decided to write/edit, or attack the tenacious weeds. Needless to say, the crabgrass usually won.

Forward to October, 2022 and my ninetieth birthday with a lovely party. It was an honor to see those with whom I have shared decades of memories, and new friends enriching my life in Hapeville. This two and a half square mile town with two busy rail lines through its center (and in front of my address on N. Central Avenue) was in the bosom of the world's busiest airport. My east-facing windows provided an approach view of three major landing strips at Atlanta's Hartsfield-Jackson International Airport. My second source of visual enjoyment came from the rolling graffiti on the trains passing in front of my house. If you are getting a picture of an elderly lady watching the world from her windows and porches, it would not be accurate. Those are incidental pleasures sandwiched between concerts in the park across the street, live performances and avant-garde movies at the restored 1920s movie theater. And, most importantly, a cadre of new friends.

My outlook became even more progressive in two areas: politics and religion. I expected to attend the beautiful Episcopal Church two miles distant in College Park. "A funny thing happened on the way to church," when I visited the Village Church, a three-minute walk, and heard Ray Waters preach. I became a regular at "The Church for Everybody" where the congregation truly represents our country and its human plethora. I left every service feeling I had a map to a better way of being.

The political realm was much more complicated, harder to understand. When the foibles, the tax and business cheating, the treatment of women by Donald Trump were revealed I thought there was no way the country would elect him to the highest position on Earth. I failed to see the racism, homophobia, the anti-Semitic, and numberless hate groups popping up from under their hiding places, feeling they had a savior in Trump. His words and actions were interpreted—by those who didn't choose to be informed—as permission to be their worst selves. Trump's sycophants, behaving as he wanted, put democracy on a path to failure I feared. Those same people adopted the "big lie" Trump spread that the election was stolen from him. Politicians who didn't want to be thrown off the gravy train, some of the super-rich who didn't want to pay their share of taxes, minions everywhere, and "good people" who claimed to be Christians but didn't live like Christians were in the ranks of his followers. There were good citizens who voted for Trump who voiced the idea they "Held their nose and cast their vote to keep the party strong."

I feared a way of life, serving well more than 250 years, was under attack from the high and mighty, the selfish, and the ill-informed. The founding fathers were amazingly prescient: Benjamin Franklin: "It's a republic if you can keep it." Thomas Jefferson: "Democracy depends on an informed electorate." The USA holds the record of the longest lasting continuous Democracy and I hope it continues for those who follow us.

In 1956 Nikita Khrushchev boldly stated, "We do not have to invade the U.S. We will take America from within." His divide and conquer thinking came to mind as rioters invaded the U.S. Capitol in an effort to install 'their' unelected president. Trump repeatedly and proudly stated his admiration for Putin, Kim Jong-un, and other all-powerful strong-man dictators.

Friends and relatives disagree vehemently over Trump, causing fissures, turning their backs on learning the truth about history in the making. Sadly, there is isolation, anger, and a host of hard feelings creating a bridge too far for some. I try to have sympathy for those who don't read accurate accounts or listen to historians, philosophers, theologians, or other learned writers who bring truth and understanding to innuendo and dangerous lies. With untamed hate, murder, and other crimes too rampant, I wonder what kind of world my great-grandson and all the children will inherit. Perhaps the world is going to be better; it appears we have hit the basement of morality.

The wise words of Martin Luther King, Jr. gave me hope, "The arc of the morality universe is long but it bends toward justice."

I admire Jimmy and Rosalynn Carter for many things including the high moral standards they set for themselves and others from the Statehouse to the White House. Most recently I applauded Jimmy's thoughtful decision to spend his final weeks at home with family instead of in an austere hospital room. He lived a life of kindness, gentility, leadership, and true Christian values. He was the most powerful person on Earth and he earned recognition as Aaron Copland's Fanfare for the Common Man. It was my exceptional luck to be a friend.

I was not as politically pessimistic as these words might seem. I continued to contribute, put up yard signs, and write notes focusing on campaigns of progressives who exhibited faith in the Constitution and believed in the innate goodness of the majority of Americans. For most of my ninety years, gardening kept me centered on action that mattered; even the crabgrass had its role. I hope I lived in a way that those who knew me said, "She left the places she touched a little better because she cared."

I should have told more friends how much I loved them and how they enriched my life.

I can't believe how fast time passed or the number of unfinished items still on my "To Do" list. No rocking chair or knitting needles for me; I didn't have time for such activities when I was young and certainly not now with only a handful of days to complete a lot of plans.

I became the person I was—good or not so good—due to examples set by a large and loving family: Taylor, Sweat, Carter, Jordan—the progenitors we knew about, who came to America from Ireland, Scotland, England and The Netherlands. I admired them for making a great choice for their families while I regretted the treatment of the Native Americans and, later, of the enslaved Africans. Perhaps new generations will discover a way to make amends for the sins of the fathers and mothers and create a just world for all. I am confident of the wisdom of the young and the universality of God's love for all creation.

About the Author

Photo by Bill Harbin.

Norma Jeanne Taylor, born October 19, 1932, at Kirkland's Turpentine Distillery where the railroad crossed U.S. 1, north of Dixie Union, Ga. Her love of education began at four and never ended. At age 75 she returned to Berry College to finish the college degree begun at age 16. Marriage—twice—motherhood and community volunteer service followed (often with her children in tow).

By appointment of Governor Carter, she became chair of the Georgia Commission on the Status of Women, worked for passage of the Equal Rights Amendment and equality in access to state medical and law schools where quotas for women were imposed. President Carter appointed her to the White House

Conference on Families for 18 months of intense volunteer work on the interchange between Federal policies and families. When reports were completed, recommendations filed, Jeanne decided enough volunteering and she started a business with a partner.

For 12 years she ran AFS, Advanced Fitness Systems, buying out her partner after the first six months. After years of six-day work weeks, she was happy to sell when approached by a chain store operation. It was back to volunteering for good causes and restoring failing houses with good bones. She is in another historic house in the shadow of the world's busiest airport. Active in the political scene, yard signs in place, postcards written, Jeanne looks forward to a future of promise for all. Her children worry about her driving in Atlanta's notorious traffic. She says put your foot on the gas pedal, close your eyes and go. Actually, in 80+ years of driving she was never given a citation until October, 2024.